RECIPES AND CONTENT COMPILED BY:
HOLLY TUDOR, FELIX CROSSE AND JENNY MCPHEE

THE ALCHEMIST
COCKTAIL BOOK

Master the dark arts of mixology

EBURY
PRESS

CONTENTS

INTRODUCTION

"All the world's a stage,
And all the men and women
merely players"

WILLIAM SHAKESPEARE
AS YOU LIKE IT, ACT II, SCENE VII

The world is a peculiar old place and life comes at you pretty quickly. Occasionally, it's good to stop and marvel at all its mystical wonder. And if all the world is, in fact, a stage, then let's inject a dash of theatre and have a little fun along the way.

So, let's play on, players, and begin by setting the scene. The Alchemist began many moons ago, bubbling up in Manchester in 2010 as a molecularly mad bar and restaurant. Drinks were served in all manner of vessels and cocktails were crafted with an obsessive eye for detail. Bedazzling and bewitching, they charged the senses for everything that followed …

If you've ever visited an Alchemist bar and taken a front row seat for the show, you'll remember the performance: bartenders wielding flaming beakers of bubbling brews, plumes of smoke and an array of colourful cocktail concoctions that play with the senses. So much more than smoke and mirrors, our 'Light-Bulb Moment' cocktails changed everything from flavour and colour to people's lives. 'Theatre Served' was born.

There are many definitions of what an alchemist does, and while we'll keep trying to turn base metal into gold, we like this one best: an alchemist is *someone who transforms things for the better*. A great example of this is our bestselling cocktail, the Smokey Old Fashioned.

There is, of course, method to our magic, and every Alchemist bartender goes through weeks of complex training to comprehend the craft — we want their performance and your experience to be exceptional every time. We want the same thing today as we did that first day: for every drink you order to be delicious, consistent and spellbinding. We find inspiration everywhere, and every drink on our menu is the result of a lot of research, trial and error, teamwork and explosions.

Over the past decade, we reckon we've concocted a thousand different drinks and every one of them tells a story. While that's definitely too many to fit in to one book, we've picked out some of our favourite tipple-y tales, so you can tell them at home. Your cocktail journey will take you through some weird and wonderful ingredients — and make sure you have those goggles at the ready, because we're going to show you some serious science along the way.

Are you ready to become an Alchemist?

EQUIPMENT

THE MODERN ALCHEMIST'S KIT BAG

BAR BLADE

A bar blade is no ordinary bottle opener: it is a speed opener, allowing you to open ten bottles of beer in 4.2 seconds (with practise!) We use it as a mark of seniority: as a bartender works through our progression scheme, they earn a personalised Alchemist bar blade, each with its own unique number.

BOSTON TIN & GLASS COCKTAIL SHAKER

We choose to create our cocktails using a Boston tin and glass shaker, rather than a tin-on-tin shaker, as we like to add a dash of theatre to everything we do. It means that, whether your cocktail is shaken or stirred, you're always able to witness a glimpse of the production.

When it comes to 'the art of the shake', build your ingredients into the glass, then slide on the tin at a slight angle and twist slightly while pushing down to seal. Hold the bottom of the glass securely with one hand while holding the top of the tin with the other. Sling the tin in one rapid motion over your shoulder and back down to lock (an added bonus is that this makes you look pretty cool). Turn the shaker upside down so the glass is facing upwards, then shake.

To unlock the tin, make sure the glass is facing upwards and use the palm of your hand to gently smack the tin where it meets the glass.

HAWTHORNE STRAINER & FINE STRAINER

Two of the most essential pieces of equipment for any bartender, place your Hawthorne strainer in the top of your Boston tin, with the coil facing downwards, and use it to hold back the ice as you strain your shaken cocktail into your glass. If your shaken cocktails are being served straight up (without ice), use in combination with a fine strainer to remove any ice shards or pulp.

BAR SPOON

The bar spoon is the crème de la crème of spoons. The long spiralled handle makes light work of mixing drinks, even in the tallest glassware, and the flat end works perfectly for layering spirits in cocktails to help you show off some artistic flair. What's more, a bar spoon holds about 5ml of liquid (the same as a teaspoon) so it can be used to measure out those smaller amounts of liquid which can be difficult to accurately do in a shot glass.

MUDDLER

We use a muddler for mashing, grinding or crushing ingredients such as fruit, herbs or spices. Essentially, this breaks them down, releasing their juices, oils and flavour compounds.

JULEP STRAINER

After stirring drinks in the glass part of your Boston shaker, use a julep strainer as you transfer the drink into your glass. Place the strainer, curved side up, over the ice (the glass should be almost full to the brim with ice) and hold it down with your index finger as you pour.

BLENDER

A good-quality blender is an important piece of equipment in any bartender's arsenal. Whether you are prepping batches or foams, or simply blending up a strawberry daiquiri on a hot summer's day, it's important to make sure you have a high-powered blender to help get the job done.

We use blenders in different ways to get different results. Blending with a scoop of crushed ice will create a frozen cocktail, while blending with three ice cubes will help to dilute the cocktail slightly, while creating a fluffy texture and velvety mouthfeel.

BLOWTORCH

A useful piece of equipment, whether you use it to torch a cinnamon stick for a sweet and spicy aroma, to caramelise a lime or to toast a meringue foam garnish. There's something about adding fire to any situation that always gives that 'wow' factor and is a guaranteed crowd-pleaser.

FOAMER

We create our foams using an iSi foamer and N_2O gas, which allows us to create velvety and stiff-peaked foams.

CHEAT'S TIP

While some cocktail enthusiasts may already own a foamer, it's not necessary. You can create your own foam at home using a hand blender or electric whisk and a piping bag.

ULTRA-PRECISION SCALES

One of the most important pieces of equipment we use on a daily basis is a set of good-quality, ultra-precision scales, accurate to the nearest 0.01g. Many of the powders we use are extremely powerful in small quantities and a variation of just 0.1g can change a drink drastically, so it's important to be accurate. You can pick up a set of these scales fairly easily online and they are generally inexpensive, so definitely worth the investment.

SMOKE GUNS

A smoke gun is an amazing piece of equipment which allows us to create thick, flavourful smoke which is perfect for infusing cocktails while creating a sense of theatre. We use oak woodchips, which give a classic smoky flavour and aroma, but you can experiment with other types of woodchips in order to get different results.

Pour the woodchips into the hole in the top of the smoke gun and turn it on to full. Direct the nozzle into the glass you want to smoke and use a lighter or match to light the woodchips. Smoke will start to billow from the nozzle. Turn off the smoker once you have achieved the desired amount of smoke, and discard the woodchips.

CREATING SMOKE WITHOUT A GUN

LIGHT SMOKE

Place some woodchips on a heat-resistant surface, such as a baking tray. Light them using a lighter flame or blowtorch until they are gently smouldering. Place your glass over the smouldering chips and leave to infuse for a few minutes. This process will lightly coat the glass with smoke and create a wonderful smoky flavour.

HEAVY SMOKE

Place the woodchips on a heat-resistant surface, such as a baking tray. Light them using a lighter flame or blowtorch until gently smouldering. Take a carafe or a stirring jar and place it over the top of the chips. Allow to infuse for a few minutes, then continue to mix the cocktail in the carafe or jar.

CHEAT'S TIP

Smoked water droplets can be added to drinks and food to create a wonderful smoky taste without woodchips or a smoke gun. Find suppliers in the resources section (→ PAGE 176).

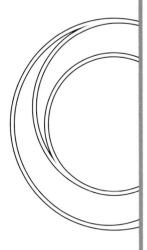

DRY ICE

Unlike other chemicals, dry ice has no liquid stage, going straight from a solid to a gas. This means it interacts with our delicious liquids in interesting ways. The process by which dry ice changes to a gas is known as sublimation. The gas it makes comes in the form of a mysterious white fog, but there are a number of magical reasons we use it in addition to its visual impact.

AROMA

When you introduce dry ice to a warm liquid infused with fresh fruit the gas carries the aroma and envelops the room. Visually, it impresses, but it's also a multi-sensory experience that gets you salivating as your drink is made.

CARBONATION

Fizzy drinks are carbonated with CO_2. The addition of dry ice to a drink lightly carbonates it, changing the mouthfeel, and alters the flavour, adding the acidity you encounter in sparkling drinks.

pH

Because of this acidity, the addition of dry ice can change a drink's pH. Depending on the ingredients, this could lead to the drink changing colour before your very eyes …

TEMPERATURE

A warm liquid reacts more quickly with dry ice, producing more aroma and fog. Dry ice is also a way of chilling the liquid without diluting it or changing the flavour in the way normal ice does.

SAFETY

You must not drink the dry ice; allow it to dissolve and dissipate first. Do not breathe dry ice mist in directly and always handle the pellets with gloves.

Do not store dry ice in a sealed container, or a freezer, but in the container provided by the manufacturer.

ELEMENTS

BASIC ESSENTIALS

STORE CUPBOARD ESSENTIALS FOR
THE MODERN ALCHEMIST

Welcome to the salt and pepper, oil and vinegar, spices and seasonings of your cocktail cabinet. Featured in this section are all the formulations for what we use here at The Alchemist to give your cocktails a certain pizzazz and take them to another level. Start by rustling up a batch of L&G; it's the most important one in our book as we use it as a swap-in for lemon juice to give a certain acidity and touch of sweetness. Once it's ready, you're all set to go on about half the cocktails here…and that's not a bad start by any means!

ALGINATE MIX
Sodium alginate is a product extracted from algae which, when combined with water, forms a gel-like substance which can be used to create our caviar and jelly spheres.

MAKES 750ML
5g sodium alginate powder
750ml filtered water

Place the ingredients in a blender and blend for 30 seconds, or until there are no lumps. This will keep in the fridge for up to 4 days.

CALCIUM SOLUTION
This dilution can be used as a calcium bath during the spherification process in our Garden Caviar recipe as well as forming an important ingredient in the Caviar One. → PAGE 140

MAKES 750ML
12g calcium lactate powder
750ml filtered water

Place the ingredients in a blender and blend for 30 seconds, or until the powder is completely dissolved. It will keep for 3 days in the fridge.

CITRIC ACID DILUTION

This dilution works well for adding a citrus element to a drink without the cloudiness that you get from lemon or lime juice.

MAKES 750ML
20g citric acid powder
750ml filtered water

Place the ingredients in a blender and blend for 30 seconds, or until the powder is completely dissolved. It will keep for at least a month, which makes it a great alternative to fresh citrus when you don't need to use it right away. Store in the fridge.

L & G *(pictured overleaf)*

Our L&G recipe is essentially a twist on a much older recipe called Oleo Saccharum, which bartenders have been using since the early 19th century to get the most out of their citrus fruits while adding extra flavour and aroma to their cocktails. The technique consists of muddling sugar into citrus peels and leaving it for a few hours or overnight, allowing the sugar to extract the oils from the peels and creating a delicious syrup. We've added lemon juice as well as bitters, creating a cocktail ingredient that packs a real punch.

MAKES 750ML
20g finely grated lemon zest or peel
500ml freshly squeezed lemon juice (around 15 large lemons)
200g caster sugar
5ml (1 teaspoon) lemon bitters

Place the lemon zest or peel in a large jug. Pour the lemon juice over the zest and leave to infuse for at least 30 minutes.
After infusing, add the caster sugar and lemon bitters and stir to dissolve. Once all of the sugar has dissolved, you can strain through a fine strainer to remove the zest, and pour the liquid into a sterilised bottle. It will keep for 4 days in the fridge.

VEGAN FOAMER

This optional foamer can be used in place of egg whites when creating foamy drinks. It has little to no taste or aroma.

MAKES 500ML
¼ teaspoon methocel
¼ teaspoon xanthan gum
500ml boiling water

Place all the ingredients in a blender and blend until smooth. Transfer to a clean bottle. It will keep for at least 7 days stored in the fridge.

Use 25ml per drink to create that fluffy egg-white texture.

SYRUPS

We recommend the Bristol Syrup Company and Monin for a good selection of flavoured syrups. See Resources → PAGE 176.

FOAMS

These extraordinary, theatrical toppings may look like a science experiment but fortunately you don't need a chemistry degree to accomplish what we do in the bars. Arm yourself with a hand blender and piping bag and follow the recipe carefully. Once you've nailed it, it will be a piece of cake to make. Kick off your education by starting with our white chocolate foam – it's the one we use the most – then work your way through the rest as your confidence grows…

These foams will all keep for 4 days inside a foamer in the fridge, or 2-3 days in an airtight container in the fridge.

When using a foamer, always follow the manufacturer's instructions.

WHITE CHOCOLATE FOAM
MAKES 500ML
350ml whipping cream
50ml whole milk
100ml white chocolate syrup

With a 500ml foamer:
Stir all the ingredients together in a jug until well combined, then pour into the foamer. Put on the lid and secure tightly.

Charge the foamer with a N_2O charge and shake well before using.

Without a foamer:
Stir all the ingredients together in a large mixing bowl until well combined. Use an electric whisk to whip the mixture until it forms stiff peaks. Carefully transfer this mixture into a piping bag with a nozzle and refrigerate until ready to use.

MERINGUE FOAM

MAKES 500ML

165ml pasteurised egg whites
165ml vanilla syrup
165ml filtered water
1 teaspoon Ultratex powder

With a 500ml foamer:
Place all the ingredients in a jug and stir well to combine. Make sure there are no lumps. Pour the mixture into the foamer, secure the lid tightly and charge with 2 × N$_2$O charges. Shake well before using. Test the meringue foam before using in a drink: if it doesn't form stiff peaks, then charge again with one more N$_2$O charge.

Without a foamer:
Place all the ingredients in a large mixing bowl and stir well to combine. Make sure there are no lumps. Use an electric whisk to whip the mixture until it forms stiff peaks. Carefully transfer this mixture into a piping bag with a nozzle and refrigerate until ready to use.

ESPRESSO FOAM

MAKES 500ML

400ml filtered water
75ml pasteurised egg whites or Vegan Foamer → PAGE 15
1 teaspoon good-quality instant coffee
25ml Simple Sugar Syrup → PAGE 28

With a 500ml foamer:
Place all the ingredients in a large jug and stir well to combine. Pour into the foamer, secure the lid tightly and charge with a N$_2$O charge. Shake well before using.

Without a foamer:
Place all the ingredients in a mixing bowl and stir well to combine. Use an electric whisk to whip the mixture until it forms stiff peaks. Carefully transfer this mixture into a piping bag with a nozzle and refrigerate until ready to use.

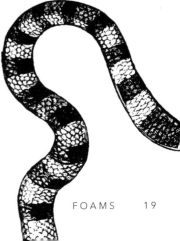

LAVENDER FOAM

MAKES 400ML

125ml lavender syrup
125ml filtered water
25ml lemon juice
125ml pasteurised egg whites or Vegan
Foamer → PAGE 15
5ml (1 teaspoon) soy lecithin

With a 500ml foamer:
Place all the ingredients in a large jug and
stir well to combine, making sure there
are no lumps. Pour into the foamer, secure
the lid tightly and charge with a N_2O charge.
Shake well before using.

Without a foamer:
Place all the ingredients in a mixing bowl
and stir well to combine, making sure there
are no lumps. Use an electric whisk to whip
the mixture until it forms stiff peaks. Carefully
transfer this mixture into a piping bag with a
nozzle and refrigerate until ready to use.

MAPLE FOAM

MAKES 450ML

120ml maple syrup
180ml filtered water
120ml pasteurised egg whites or Vegan
Foamer → PAGE 15
30ml lemon juice
5ml (1 teaspoon) soy lecithin

With a 500ml foamer:
Place all the ingredients in a large jug and
stir well to combine, making sure there are
no lumps. Pour into the foamer, secure the lid
tightly and charge with a N_2O charge. Shake
well before using.

Without a foamer:
Place all the ingredients in a mixing bowl
and stir well to combine, making sure there
are no lumps. Use an electric whisk to whip
the mixture until it forms stiff peaks. Carefully
transfer this mixture into a piping bag with
a nozzle and refrigerate until ready to use.

SPIRIT BATCHES
& INFUSIONS

Take your cocktail creations to another level and learn, here in this chapter, how to infuse interesting flavour into spirits. Throw in just a few additions – think banana, cardamom and tropical tinctures – and a little bit of time, to create a magical boost that will step up your mixology game.

FLAVOUR-CHANGING MIX

The magic ingredient in the Flavour Changing One (→ PAGE 131), this mix uses xanthan gum to change the density of the liquid causing the mix to sink in the cocktail and give the impression that the drink is changing flavour.

MAKES 650ML

250ml filtered water
200ml crème de menthe blanc (white mint) liqueur
100ml crème de cacao blanc (white chocolate) liqueur
100ml white chocolate syrup
¼ teaspoon xanthan gum

Place all the ingredients in a blender and blend to combine. Transfer to a sterilised bottle and place in the fridge. Allow it to settle for a few hours before using.

CARDAMOM GIN *(pictured overleaf)*
This infusion adds a herbaceous or vegetal taste and aroma to your cocktails and is the star ingredient in the Legal One (→ PAGE 139).

MAKES 700ML
700ml gin
4 cardamom leaves

Add the leaves to the gin bottle and leave to infuse for at least 24 hours. If you need to infuse it faster, you can slightly warm the gin in order to speed up the process. After 24 hours, remove the leaves from the bottle.

BANANA VERMOUTH
This infusion is a fresh take on a classic, and the star of the show in our iconic Bananagroni (→ PAGE 95).

MAKES 700ML
4 bananas
700ml Martini Ambrato vermouth or other white vermouth

Peel and chop the bananas into thin slices, around 5mm thick. Lay out the slices on a baking sheet lined with baking paper and place in a dehydrator or oven at 55°C. Leave in the dehydrator or oven for 12 hours to dehydrate.

Pour the vermouth into a large jar and add the dried bananas. Cover and leave to soak for 12 hours.

Strain the liquid to remove the bananas, making sure to squeeze out every drop of vermouth. Pour the vermouth into a sterilised bottle.

TROPICAL VERMOUTH
This infusion adds a tropical and zesty touch to any cocktail without diluting it down.

MAKES 700ML
24 citrus wedges (we use leftover fruit from our chopping boards to avoid waste)
700ml Martini Ambrato vermouth or other white vermouth
½ teaspoon pineapple flavour drops

Chop the fruit into wedges, around 1cm thick. Lay out the slices on a baking sheet lined with baking paper and place in an dehyrdrator or oven at 55°C/gas mark ⅛. Leave in the dehydrator or oven for 12 hours to dehydrate.

Pour the vermouth into a large jar and stir in the pineapple flavour drops. Add the dehydrated fruit, then cover and leave to soak for 12 hours.

Strain the vermouth to remove the fruit, then pour into a sterilised bottle.

ZOMBIE MIX
This mix is what gives our Dead Red Zombie (→ PAGE 87) cocktail its boozy finish. Prepping this batch will help to accurately portion the absinthe and maraschino in the cocktail.

MAKES 700ML
400ml Grande Absente absinthe
300ml maraschino cherry liqueur

Pour both the ingredients into a large jug and stir well to mix.

SHRUBS & SYRUPS

The time-honoured method of preserving fruit juice with sugar and acid is sometimes referred to as 'drinking vinegars' but also runs under the banner of shrubs. Now, with a wide variety of fruit and vinegars, herbs and spices available at our fingertips, the world's our oyster in the combinations of flavours we can create. The best ones are the perfect balance between sweet and tart. Not only are they a staple base for us, they're also a great way to use up leftover fruit from garnishes that would otherwise be heading for the bin.

Syrups, in contrast, offer pure sweetness and also deliver a certain viscosity to cocktails. A simple sugar syrup is your starting base, then swap in different ingredients to suit the occasion and produce the varying flavour required.

SIMPLE SUGAR SYRUP (GOMME)

The most prevalent syrup in your back bar, you'll use this in most classic cocktail recipes.

MAKES 700ML
350g caster sugar
350ml boiling water

Place the sugar and water in a small saucepan over a medium heat. Stir continuously until all the sugar is dissolved, then transfer into a clean bottle. Leave to cool before using.

This syrup will keep for at least a month in the fridge.

WINTER SUGAR SYRUP (GOMME)

This is a wintery twist on a simple sugar syrup. Demerara adds caramel notes while coffee, cinnamon and vanilla create a warming taste and aroma which works perfectly in our Smokey No.2 (→ PAGE 90).

MAKES 700ML

350g demerara sugar
8 espresso coffee beans
3 cinnamon sticks
350ml filtered water
5ml (1 teaspoon) vanilla bean paste

Place all the ingredients in a small saucepan over a medium heat and stir continuously until the sugar is dissolved. Carefully pour the mixture into a jar or tub and leave to infuse for 2 days at room temperature. After 2 days, strain to remove the solid ingredients and transfer to a clean bottle.

This will keep for at least a month in the fridge.

CITRUS & MINT SHRUB

(see previous spread)

We created this shrub in an effort to find a way to use up leftover chopping-board fruit that would otherwise be thrown away at the end of the night. The combination of citrus, mint and apple cider vinegar creates a fresh and invigorating cordial which works brilliantly in alcoholic drinks and makes for a more sophisticated non-alcoholic offering.

MAKES 300ML

3 oranges
3 pink grapefruits
100g fresh mint leaves
200g caster sugar
100ml apple cider vinegar

Peel the oranges and grapefruits, then cut them into segments and place them in a large bowl or tub. Muddle the fruit to release the juices.

Add the mint, then cover the mixture with the caster sugar. Mix thoroughly and leave to rest at room temperature for at least 2 hours.

Now add the cider vinegar and stir well to combine. Leave to rest for another hour, then strain to remove the fruit and mint. You should be left with a syrup. Transfer this to a clean bottle and refrigerate until ready to use.

This will keep for at least a month.

MALT SYRUP

Malt extract is incredibly thick and can be difficult to use in small measurements, so combining it with water allows us to portion it much more easily for use in a cocktail.

MAKES 700ML
350ml malt extract
350ml warm water

Place the malt extract and warm water in a blender and blend to combine. Transfer to a clean bottle and allow to settle before using. Store in the fridge until ready to use.

This will keep for at least a month.

FIRE SYRUP

This batch is what gives our Dead Red Zombie (→ PAGE 87) cocktail its signature shimmer. Combining with syrup and water helps us to easily portion the ruby powder into each cocktail.

MAKES 750ML
275ml passionfruit syrup
275ml raspberry syrup
1 teaspoon ruby metallic powder
1½ teaspoons Ultratex powder
200ml boiling water

Place the passionfruit syrup, raspberry syrup and ruby powder in a blender and blend to combine.

In a jug, mix together the Ultratex powder and boiling water and stir until smooth. Pour this mixture into the syrup mixture and stir well to combine. Transfer to a clean bottle.

This will keep for at least a month in the fridge.

RED MIX

MAKES 700ML
1 teaspoon red colouring powder
700ml filtered water
¼ teaspoon xanthan gum

Place all the ingredients in a blender and blend to combine until smooth with no lumps. Transfer to a clean bottle and refrigerate until ready to serve.

This will keep for at least a month.

BERGAMOT DILUTION

MAKES 330ML
1 dash of bergamot flavour drops
80ml Simple Sugar Syrup → PAGE 28
250ml filtered water

Blend all ingredients together and transfer to a clean bottle.

This dilution should keep for at least a month in the fridge.

SPHERIFICATION

Our caviars of the cocktail world create an eye-catching addition to any drink. These little balls are a chemical reaction produced by dropping sodium alginate (a molecule found in seaweed) into a calcium solution to create the small squishy spheres. These can be a bit of a challenge but once you've mastered the technique, the possibilities are endless. Once you've made the base, the world's your oyster as we show you how to add a myriad of flavour. Rhubarb Caviar, calling on just a handful of ingredients, is a great place to start if you're looking for simplicity. Then graduate to the Garden Caviar, scented with mint, which requires a little bit more skill.

RHUBARB CAVIAR

The star ingredient for The Caviar One (→ PAGE 140), make this ahead of time and refrigerate until you're ready to make cocktails.

MAKES 250ML

50ml rhubarb purée
150ml Alginate Mix → PAGE 14
50ml grenadine syrup
0.22g red colouring powder

Combine all the ingredients together in a bowl and stir well to mix. Transfer to a clean bottle and keep refrigerated until ready to use. This caviar will keep for at least 4 days when refrigerated.

To see how to use this caviar mixture in a cocktail, see → PAGE 140.

GOLD VANILLA SPHERES

(see previous spread)

These are made using a process called reverse spherification. Like spherification, this process uses sodium alginate and calcium lactate to create jelly spheres. However, by reversing the process, we are able to create larger spheres with a liquid centre which you can pop with a spoon or straw. For these golden orbs, we've taken the process one step further by encapsulating 24-carat edible gold flakes inside the jelly sphere, which gives that extra 'wow' factor. If you can't get hold of these gold flakes, it works just as well without them.

MAKES 7 SPHERES
2 teaspoons calcium lactate powder
60ml boiling water
150ml vanilla syrup
90ml filtered water
24-carat edible gold sheet flakes
700ml Alginate Mix → PAGE 14
You will also need 7 × petit four moulds,
7 × rocks glasses and a food thermometer

In a jug, mix together the calcium lactate powder and boiling water until the powder has dissolved. Careful, this will be hot. Add the vanilla syrup, filtered water and gold flakes, and stir to combine, ensuring the gold is evenly distributed. Divide the mixture between the petit four moulds. Transfer them to the freezer and freeze for 4 hours or until completely frozen.

Once they are frozen, heat the alginate mix in a saucepan until it reaches 70°C. Pour 100ml of the mixture into each rocks glass.

Drop one frozen gold sphere into each glass of alginate and allow it to sink to the bottom. After about a minute, a jelly skin should begin to form around the ball. Wait for 3 minutes, then carefully strain out the spheres.

Put the first jelly sphere straight into a bowl of warm water to wash off any excess alginate, then do the same with the other 6 spheres.

Store the gold spheres in a jar with 250ml water and refrigerate for up to a week until ready to serve.

GARDEN CAVIAR

(see previous spread)

MAKES 835ML
560ml filtered water
125ml Simple Sugar Syrup → PAGE 28
½ teaspoon garden mint flavour drops
1 teaspoon sodium alginate powder
0.22g green colouring powder
10 fresh mint leaves
150ml Calcium Solution → PAGE 14

Place all the ingredients except the mint and calcium solution in a blender and blend to combine. Strain through a fine strainer into a tub or jug. Add the mint leaves and leave to infuse for 20 minutes, then strain again to remove the leaves.

To make the caviar, pour the calcium solution into a bowl and use a syringe or pipette to drop small droplets of the caviar mixture into the calcium bath. The droplets will start to form tiny jelly spheres. Wait 30 seconds for the spheres to form, then strain out and serve.

GARNISHES

Just like a shower of cheese over the perfect bolognese or a dusting of icing sugar on top of a light-as-air sponge, garnishes complete the drinks in the same way that they finish off a feast in culinary terms. Each cocktail is a work of art in itself and these last little touches tie it all together. It's key to play on the flavours in each drink and match the garnish to those so, as we say, 'it makes sense' in the cocktail. To ease you in, try your hand at the Orchid Ice Ball to add a wow-factor flourish to a White Cosmo.

ORANGE GLASS (pictured overleaf)
The famous flourish on our Chocolate Orange Smasherac (→ PAGE 92).

MAKES 10-15
450g isomalt
2½ teaspoons orange flavour drops
You will also need round, heat-proof disc-shaped silicone moulds. Ours are 15cm, but you can use any size large enough to sit on top of your glass.

Place the isomalt in a small saucepan over a medium heat and stir until it melts down. Add the orange flavour drops.

Once melted, turn off the heat and allow the mixture to cool slightly for 30 seconds. Careful, this will be very hot. Then pour into the moulds. Wait 30 minutes for the mixture to cool, then carefully move the moulds around to allow even coverage.

Transfer to the fridge for 3 hours to cool and set. Once set, carefully remove the orange glass. Store in an airtight container, separated by sheets of baking paper. These are incredibly fun to smash!

BOOZY PINEAPPLE JELLY

The jelly that gives our Pot o' Gold cocktail its name, this is a light-hearted take on the jello shots of yester year. We also use a gelatin alternative which makes these jellies vegetarian, an added bonus!

MAKES 450ML

150ml filtered water
50ml pineapple juice
50ml Citric Acid Dilution → PAGE 15
100ml pineapple and coconut syrup
½ teaspoon pineapple flavour drops
0.6g yellow colouring powder
20g caster sugar
7.5g MSK UltraGel 2
50ml pineapple gin
50ml white rum
You will also need 18-20 shot glasses

Place the water, pineapple juice, citric acid dilution, pineapple and coconut syrup, pineapple flavour drops and yellow colouring powder in a large saucepan over a medium heat. Stir well to combine and warm through for about 5 minutes, or until visibly warm but not boiling.

In a small bowl, mix together the caster sugar and UltraGel until combined. Mixing them together first will help the gelling powder to disperse better in the liquid and avoid lumps forming.

When the liquid in the saucepan is hot, slowly add the gel and sugar mixture, a little at a time, stirring continuously.

Once it's all dissolved, turn off the heat and quickly pour in the gin and rum, stirring to mix. Allow the mix to cool.

Pour the mixture into the shot glasses and place them in the fridge for at least 3 hours to set.

ORCHID ICE BALL *(pictured overleaf)*

An easy way to instantly transform a cocktail, boosting its Instagram-ability.

MAKES 1

1 fresh orchid flower
filtered water
You will also need a small ice-ball mould

Add the orchid to the ice-ball mould and fill with water. Place in the freezer for at least 4 hours or until frozen through. Keep in the freezer until ready to serve.

To serve, simple add the ice ball to your chosen glass and pour your drink over the top.

DEHYDRATED FRUIT

We like to use discarded chopping board fruit which would otherwise go to waste to make dehydrated fruit garnishes as well as infusions.

To make, chop the fruit into wedges or slices, around 1cm thick. Lay out the slices on a baking sheet lined with baking paper and place in an dehyrdrator or oven at 55°C/gas mark ⅛. Leave in the dehydrator or oven for 12 hours to dehydrate.

When fully dehydrated, transfer to a jar and seal to ensure they keep dry.

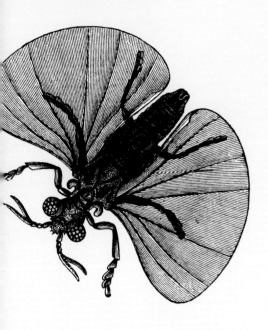

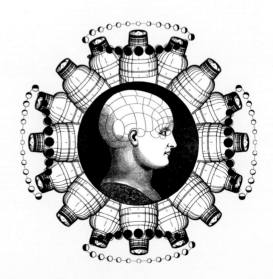

COCKTAILS

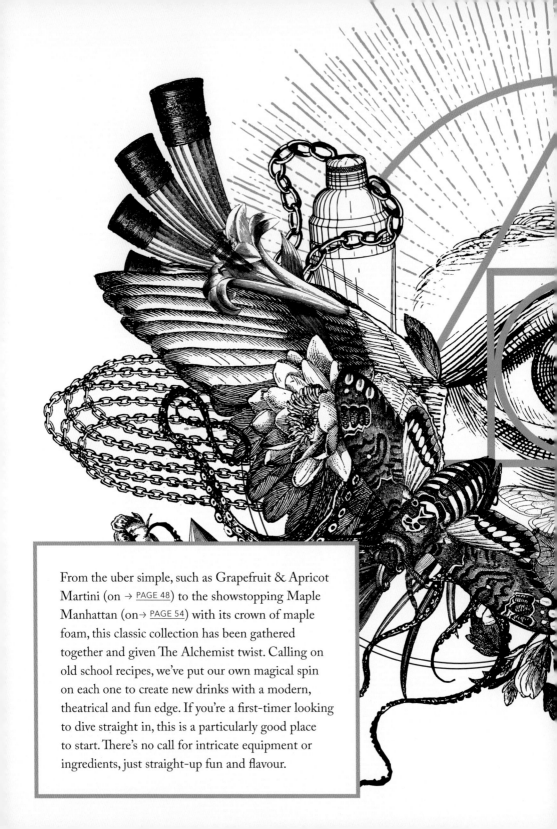

From the uber simple, such as Grapefruit & Apricot Martini (on → PAGE 48) to the showstopping Maple Manhattan (on→ PAGE 54) with its crown of maple foam, this classic collection has been gathered together and given The Alchemist twist. Calling on old school recipes, we've put our own magical spin on each one to create new drinks with a modern, theatrical and fun edge. If you're a first-timer looking to dive straight in, this is a particularly good place to start. There's no call for intricate equipment or ingredients, just straight-up fun and flavour.

TWISTED
CLASSICS

LADY MARMALADE

☛ **BREAKFAST VODKA VERMOUTH**

This twist on a breakfast martini may be a cinch to knock
up, but there's a wonderful complexity to the finished
sip, thanks to the Belsazar Red Vermouth flavoured with
unusual herbs. Go the whole hog and source dry ice for
the full showstopping finish.

MAKES 1
25ml marmalade vodka
25ml red vermouth
15ml (1 tablespoon) L&G → PAGE 15
30ml Bergamot Dilution → PAGE 30
ice cubes
5-6 pellets of dry ice
orange zest twist
grapefruit zest twist

GLASSWARE

❧

conical flask
rocks glass

- Add the vodka, vermouth, L&G and bergamot dilution
  to a small saucepan over a low heat. Simmer until
  bubbles appear.
- Add some ice cubes ice to the rocks glass, then add the
  dry ice to the conical flask and pour over the warm liquid.
- Twist the grapefruit and orange zest twists into the neck
  of the flask.
- Allow the smoke to dissipate before pouring the mixture
  over the ice cubes in the rocks glass to serve. Do not
  drink the dry ice.

WHITE COSMO

👉 **LIGHT, DELICATE, ORCHID**

A simple twist on the classic: it's citrusy, not too sweet
and very fresh. For a striking presentation, use round balls
of ice frozen with edible flowers inside.

MAKES 1
4 white grapes
25ml vodka
15ml (1 tablespoon) elderflower liqueur
5ml (1 teaspoon) Cointreau
5ml (1 teaspoon) Simple Sugar Syrup → PAGE 28
15ml (1 tablespoon) filtered water
7.5ml (½ tablespoon) fresh lime juice
15ml (1 tablespoon) Citric Acid Dilution → PAGE 15
2 dashes of lemon bitters
ice cubes
Orchid Ice Ball → PAGE 35

GLASSWARE

coupe

- Place the grapes in a Boston shaker and muddle to
  release their flavour. Pour in the vodka, elderflower
  liqueur, Cointreau, sugar syrup, water, lime juice, citric
  acid dilution and bitters.
- Add some ice to the shaker and shake for 30 seconds,
  or until condensation forms on the outside of the shaker.
- Place the orchid ice ball in your glass and strain the
  cocktail over the top using a fine strainer. Serve.

PINK FIZZ PALOMA

☞ **ZESTY, MEXICAN, FOAMY**

Pairing a bitter grapefruit liqueur with an IPA might
sound unusual, but here's why it works: the dry, hoppy
flavours of the beer match the bitterness in the grapefruit,
while the sweetness in the syrup adds balance throughout.
We recommend Pampelle for the grapefruit liquor for its
distinctive flavour.

MAKES 1
25ml tequila
25ml bitter grapefruit liqueur
1½ teaspoons Simple Sugar Syrup → PAGE 28
20ml grapefruit juice
½ teaspoon soy lecithin
ice cubes
40ml your favourite IPA
rice paper, to garnish (optional)

GLASSWARE

coupe

- Place the tequila, grapefruit liqueur, sugar syrup,
  grapefruit juice and soy lecithin in a Boston shaker with
  some ice cubes. Shake and strain into the coupe through
  a fine strainer.
- Pour over the IPA to give a velvety foam, then top
  with printed rice paper in your chosen design for an
  optional garnish.

TIP

There are plenty of places online
where you can design custom rice
papers for your drinks.

GRAPEFRUIT & APRICOT MARTINI

☞ **SWEET, SOUR PERFECTION**

This little twist on a martini has a pretty legendary status in the world of The Alchemist. Drawing on just a handful of ingredients, it's simple, refreshing and a great entry-level intro to the wonderful world of martinis. Fans of a classic G&T will love it.

MAKES 1
½ pink grapefruit
30ml gin
15ml (1 tablespoon) apricot liqueur
15ml (1 tablespoon) Simple Sugar Syrup → <u>PAGE 28</u>
ice cubes
grapefruit zest twist, to garnish

GLASSWARE

coupe

- Squeeze the grapefruit half into a Boston shaker, then add the gin, apricot liqueur and sugar syrup. Add some ice cubes and shake well. Strain through a fine strainer into a chilled coupe and serve garnished with a grapefruit zest twist.

LAVENDER DAIQUIRI

☞ **FLORAL, VIOLET, CREAM**

This fuses all the scents of a flower-filled field in midsummer with a tropical night out — and it works! Rum, pineapple, lime and coconut cream hold the whole thing together while the lavender foam tops it off, like the perfect icing on a cake.

GLASSWARE

coupe, chilled

MAKES 1

25ml white rum
25ml coconut rum
15ml (1 tablespoon) coconut cream
15ml (1 tablespoon) fresh lime juice
25ml pineapple juice
ice cubes
100ml Lavender Foam → PAGE 21
lavender sprig, to garnish

- Pour the white rum, coconut rum, coconut cream, lime juice and pineapple juice into a Boston shaker. Add some ice cubes and shake well. Strain through a fine strainer into the chilled coupe.
- Top with the lavender foam and serve, garnished with a lavender sprig.

BUBBLEGUM DAIQUIRI

☞ **HUBBA BUBBA BLEND**

Slushie's all grown up. An absolute blast from the past, it makes a great thirst-quenching choice on a hot summer's day. A scattering of popping candy finishes it off with just the right amount of kitsch.

MAKES 1
40ml white rum
15ml (1 tablespoon) fresh lime juice
20ml bubblegum syrup
5ml (1 teaspoon) grenadine
40ml apple juice
ice cubes
crushed ice, enough to fill your glass
1 teaspoon popping candy, to garnish

GLASSWARE

coupe

- Place the rum, lime juice, bubblegum syrup, grenadine and apple juice in a blender along with some ice cubes.
- Blend until smooth and pour into the glass. Garnish with popping candy just before serving.

GARDEN MARTINI

☛ **GIN, ROSE, HAPPINESS**

Come, walk with us into our spring garden and relax into this special cocktail, blooming with elderflower and lavender. We find that floral Hendrick's gin provides the best base over which to layer elderflower and rose liqueurs, followed by a splash of apple juice, and finished with lavender foam and a cucumber slice.

GLASSWARE

❧

coupe

MAKES 1
30ml gin
1½ teaspoons elderflower liqueur
1½ teaspoons rose liqueur
15ml (1 tablespoon) L&G → PAGE 15
25ml apple juice
ice cubes
100ml Lavender Foam → PAGE 21
cucumber slice, to garnish

- Pour the gin, elderflower liqueur, rose liqueur, L&G and apple juice into a Boston shaker. Add some ice cubes and shake well. Strain through a fine strainer into the coupe.
- Finish with the lavender foam and a slice of cucumber, and serve.

MAPLE MANHATTAN

☛ **SWEET, TOASTY FOAM**

A serious and delicious little tipple for accomplished cocktail lovers. Scotch and vermouth kick off the party, mingling in a Boston with some ice. Then, once this concoction has been strained into a glass, it's topped with a stunning layer of maple foam. Sip back and relax…

MAKES 1
40ml scotch
15ml (1 tablespoon) sweet vermouth
15ml (1 tablespoon) filtered water
1 dash of aromatic bitters
1 dash of orange bitters
ice cubes
100ml Maple Foam → PAGE 21
1 slice dehydrated pear, to garnish

GLASSWARE

⧗

coupe, chilled
or petri dish

- Add the scotch, sweet vermouth, water and both types of bitters to a Boston shaker with some ice cubes.
- Stir for 1 minute or until diluted slightly and strain into your glassware without the ice.
- Top with the maple foam and dehydrated pear to serve.

COLA BOTTLE LIBRE

☞ **SWEETS, COLA, RETRO**

If the classic rum and coke's your bag, this is right up your street… It's a clever twist on the brown version — this one is totally clear — calling for white rum, citrus and a dot of cola flavour to give that unmistakeable taste. Tons of ice and a chewy cola bottle sweet complete the treat.

GLASSWARE

small bottle
collins glass

MAKES 1
50ml white rum
25ml Simple Sugar Syrup → PAGE 28
50ml Citric Acid Dilution → PAGE 15
1 drop cola flavour drops
180ml soda water
ice cubes
cola bottle sweet, to garnish

- Pour the rum, sugar syrup, citric acid dilution, cola flavour drop and soda water into the glass bottle and stir until fully combined.
- Serve with a collins glass full of ice cubes, and garnish with a cola bottle sweet.

VESPER MARTINI

👉 **CLASSIC 007**

Immortalised by James Bond in *Casino Royale*, this has all the va-va voom of a classic martini and more. Our spin is ultra-boozy, loaded with lemon for extra zing. It's best served on the rocks.

MAKES 1
30ml gin
15ml (1 tablespoon) filtered water
15ml (1 tablespoon) vodka
25ml Lillet Blanc
2 dashes of lemon bitters
ice cubes
lemon zest twist, to garnish

GLASSWARE

🏺
hipflask
rocks glass

- Pour the gin, water, vodka, Lillet Blanc and bitters into a small jug. Stir and pour into a hipflask. Place the hipflask in the fridge until ready to serve.
- Serve the chilled hipflask alongside a rocks glass, filled with ice cubes, with a twist of lemon zest.

NEW WAVE

Welcome to the wonderful world of our signature
drinks. With less focus on the theatrical, these
beauties are all about the simple and the serious, the
booze and the flavour. Think Peaches & Cream (on
→ PAGE 62) with its double dose of heavenly fragrant
and fruity liqueurs and sweet nature. Or if gin's your
bag, try the very grown-up 3.5oz of Happiness (on
→ PAGE 65) calling on Tanqueray No.10, raspberry-
based Chambord and a mix of two vermouths. In
short they're all, quite simply, downright delicious.

PEACHES & CREAM

🏴 **PEACHY, CREAMY, FIZZ**

Our sophisticated take on a peach Bellini calls for two fruit-filled liqueurs — peach and grapefruit — along with the classic prosecco. There's no cream in it though. It's the magic of adding soy lecithin, which reacts with the bubbles in the fizz to produce a frothy, creamy texture. It's a lovely first drink of the night and makes a good swap for a mimosa.

MAKES 1
ice cubes
25ml crème de pêche liqueur
25ml pink grapefruit liqueur
15ml (1 tablespoon) L&G → PAGE 15
½ teaspoon soy lecithin
50ml prosecco
orange zest twist, to garnish

GLASSWARE

flute

- Fill a Boston shaker with ice cubes, then add the crème de pêche liqueur, pink grapefruit liqueur, L&G and soy lecithin. Shake well, then strain into the flute through a fine strainer.
- Top with the prosecco and garnish with an orange zest twist before serving.

MAKING MAGIC HAPPEN

The soy lecithin in this recipe reacts with the carbonation in the prosecco, creating a velvety, creamy mouthfeel.

3.5OZ
OF HAPPINESS

☛ **VERMOUTH, RASPBERRY, HAPPINESS**

This cocktail is pretty simple, and it's ideal for festivals and picnics. It can also be scaled up for an indulgent wedding favour. Our bartender's gin of choice for this has to be Tanqueray No. 10.

GLASSWARE

hipflask
rocks glass

MAKES 1
25ml gin
25ml Chambord liqueur
15ml (1 tablespoon) red vermouth
15ml (1 tablespoon) dry vermouth
15ml (1 tablespoon) Citric Acid Dilution → PAGE 15
1 dash of orange bitters
ice cubes
orange zest twist

- Combine the gin, Chambord, red vermouth, dry vermouth, citric acid dilution and orange bitters and pour into the hipflask. Refrigerate until ready to serve.
- Serve with a rocks glass full of ice cubes, and a twist of orange zest to accentuate the flavours.

BEYOND THE KALE

☞ **DRINK YOUR GREENS**

Our boozy alternative to a green smoothie features tons of kale, lots of lime juice, a dash of sugar syrup to bring it altogether and a generous measure of vodka (we use the vegetal-tasting Żubrówka vodka). A high-speed blender is recommended to get the texture good and smooth.

MAKES 1
crushed ice, enough to fill your glass
45ml vodka
25ml fresh lime juice
25ml Simple Sugar Syrup → PAGE 28
handful of torn kale, plus a large leaf, to garnish

GLASSWARE

sling glass

- Add the ice, vodka, lime juice, sugar syrup and torn kale to a high-speed blender and blend until smooth. Pour into the sling glass and serve, garnished with a large kale leaf.

FLOWER SOUR

FLORAL, JUNIPER, FUN

Violet liqueur is the cocktail guru's go-to to mimic the taste of Parma Violet sweets. It and rose liqueur run through the heart of this drink, alongside a splash of gin to balance the flavour. Apple juice, lemon and lavender foam give it a modern feel, and position it firmly within the sour section.

GLASSWARE

sling glass

MAKES 1
25ml gin
15ml (1 tablespoon) violet liqueur
15ml (1 tablespoon) rose liqueur
25ml L&G → PAGE 15
50ml apple juice
75ml Lavender Foam → PAGE 21
ice cubes
lemon wedge, to garnish

- Pour the gin, violet liqueur, rose liqueur, L&G, apple juice and lavender foam into a Boston shaker with some ice cubes.
- Shake and strain into the sling glass. Serve garnished with a lemon wedge.

MILK & HONEY

This sounds crazy, but trust us. Back before refrigeration was invented, milk was clarified in order to preserve it. We adopted the technique in this punch for a smooth, creamy texture. The boozy combination of rum and falernum conjures up a taste similar to chewy cola bottles.

MAKES 10

600ml white rum
300ml velvet falernum
150ml cinnamon syrup
150ml fresh lime juice
5 tablespoons loose-leaf chai tea
500ml whole milk

GLASSWARE

large 2L jug and bottle
rocks glasses

—

You will also need
a funnel and
a paper coffee filter

- Place the rum, falernum, cinnamon syrup, lime juice and chai tea into a saucepan and set over a high heat for 5 minutes or until warmed through.
- Meanwhile, pour the milk into a separate saucepan and warm through over a low heat – do not boil.
- Remove both pans from the heat and combine the warm milk with the punch mixture in the 2-litre jug and stir through. The mixture of milk and citrus will begin to curdle – and this is where the magic happens!
- Place the funnel over the bottle and line it with the paper coffee filter. Slowly pour over the liquid. The first few drops with come through quickly and will look cloudy while the curds settle on the filter paper. Allow this to come through. When the liquid slows to a steady drip, briefly remove the funnel from the bottle and pour the first few drops from the bottle back into the filter, before replacing the bottle underneath (filtering them twice).
- Once all the liquid has filtered through the curds you should be left with a crystal clear cocktail. You can now bottle this up and refrigerate until ready to use.

CEREAL KILLER

There's a sweet and crunchy breakfast vibe here.
A white Russian twist forms the base, with honey liqueur,
brandy, gingerbread syrup and milk. Once shaken and
poured, it's garnished with a handful of cereal hoops.
Fun and frivolous!

GLASSWARE

coupe, chilled

—

You will also need
a spoon

MAKES 1

30ml brandy
15ml (1 tablespoon) honey liqueur
15ml (1 tablespoon) Licor 43
50ml whole milk
5ml (1 teaspoon) gingerbread syrup
ice cubes
2 tablespoons cereal hoops, to garnish

- Pour the brandy, honey liqueur, Licor 43, milk and
  gingerbread syrup into a Boston shaker, along with
  some ice cubes.
- Gently shake, then strain through a fine strainer into
  the chilled coupe.
- Serve, garnished with cereal, with a spoon.

CINNAMON APPLE

☛ **AUTUMNAL, SPICED, CREAM**

Like a slice of spiced apple cake hot from the oven, this will warm your cockles on a winter's night. There's crisp apple, vodka, fresh lime juice and some gingerbread syrup, alongside sweet, aromatic spices and a touch of white chocolate foam. The special bit? A shake in the Boston blends all the ingredients together into a wonderful creamy feast.

MAKES 1

25ml vodka
25ml green apple liqueur
10ml (2 teaspoons) Simple Sugar Syrup → <u>PAGE 28</u>
10m (2 teaspoons) gingerbread syrup
15ml (1 tablespoon) fresh lime juice
25ml apple juice
50ml White Chocolate Foam → <u>PAGE 18</u>
ice cubes
pinch of ground cinnamon
pinch of ground nutmeg
cinnamon stick, to garnish

GLASSWARE

⧗

coupe, chilled

- Pour the vodka, apple liqueur, sugar syrup, gingerbread syrup, lime juice, apple juice and white chocolate foam into a Boston shaker. Add some ice cubes and shake, then strain through a fine strainer into the chilled coupe.
- Sprinkle over the ground cinnamon and nutmeg and serve garnished with a cinnamon stick.

PASSION FRUIT & LYCHEE MERINGUE MARTINI

☞ **SWEET, SUN, MERINGUE**

Have a serious sweet tooth? If so is this for you… Fruity liqueurs are topped with a crown of meringue-like foam, then dredged in sugar and torched until golden. It's gloriously messy so we recommend serving with a spoon.

MAKES 1
25ml lychee liqueur
25ml passion fruit liqueur
15ml (1 tablespoon) fresh lime juice
10ml (2 teaspoons) L&G → PAGE 15
25ml apple juice
ice cubes
100ml Meringue Foam → PAGE 19
pinch of caster sugar

GLASSWARE
⏳
coupe, chilled
—
You will also need
a blowtorch and
a spoon

- Pour the lychee liqueur, passion fruit liqueur, lime juice, L&G and apple juice into a Boston shaker, along with some ice cubes. Shake and strain into the chilled coupe.
- Top with the meringue foam and sprinkle over the sugar, then use a blowtorch (it's fire, be careful!) to caramelise the top. Serve with a spoon.

WHITE CHOC RASPBERRY

☞ **CREAMY CROWD-PLEASER**

A fruity little number, based on a chocolate truffle. Lots of creamy, fruity flavours here, but our secret ingredients — Aperol and cranberry juice — add another dimension, knocking the edge off and making sure the sweetness doesn't become too cloying.

GLASSWARE

🌿

coupe, chilled

MAKES 1
30ml raspberry vodka
10ml (2 teaspoons) Chambord liqueur
10ml (2 teaspoons) Aperol
10ml (2 teaspoons) raspberry syrup
40ml cranberry juice
ice cubes
100ml White Chocolate Foam → <u>PAGE 18</u>
crushed freeze-dried raspberries, to garnish

- Pour the raspberry vodka, Chambord, Aperol, raspberry syrup and cranberry juice into a Boston shaker and add some ice cubes. Shake and strain through a fine strainer into the chilled coupe.
- Top with the white chocolate foam and serve, garnished with crushed freeze-dried raspberries.

ROSEBUD

👉 **FLORAL, CLEAN, ROSY**

A sweet-scented, soft pink cocktail. Light and delicately flavoured, this makes a refreshing sip for when the sun comes out. The gin base, featuring aromatics of angelica and sweet liquorice, works like a dream with the rose liqueur and the hint of citrus from the L&G. Perfect for summer, and an admirable cocktail with which to kick off a wedding.

MAKES 1
crushed ice
ice cubes
40ml gin
10ml (2 teaspoons) rose liqueur
10ml (2 teaspoons) Simple Sugar Syrup → PAGE 28
15ml (1 tablespoon) L&G → PAGE 15
8 dried pink rosebuds

GLASSWARE

⧖

small milk bottle

- Fill the bottle with crushed ice.
- Fill a Boston shaker with ice cubes, then add the gin, rose liqueur, sugar syrup and L&G, along with 4 of the rosebuds.
- Shake and strain into the bottle over the crushed ice. Garnish with remaining rosebuds and serve.

AMARO MIO

CARAMELISED, LIME, SPICE

Bitter-tasting amaro, which is made by infusing
a spirit with a host of herbs and other ingredients,
forms the heart of this drink. We've built on this base
by adding rum to create flavours of chocolate and
cinnamon, along with a smattering of spice. A good
shake with wedges of caramelised lime heightens the
aromatics within.

GLASSWARE

rocks glass
–
You will also need
a blowtorch

MAKES 1
8 lime wedges
20g demerara sugar
ice cubes
25ml golden rum
25ml amaro

- Place the lime wedges in a small saucepan or baking tray
  and softly muddle, the sprinkle over the sugar and use
  a blowtorch (it's fire, be careful!) to caramelise the limes.
- Put some ice cubes in a Boston shaker, along with the
  rum, and amaro. Add the caramelised limes, shake and
  pour into the rocks glass to serve.

MILK MONEY

☞ **BREAK TIME MILK**

Get set to be transported straight back to the golden days of milk time. This retro little number features hazelnut sauce (we use the brand made by our pals at Manchester's cult café, Black Milk), and gorgeous nut and coffee liqueurs. Serve in a dinky milk bottle and stick a foil-wrapped chocolate on top for the ultimate experience.

MAKES 1
crushed ice, enough to fill your
    milk bottle ¾ full
25ml amaretto
15ml (1 tablespoon) coffee liqueur
15ml (1 tablespoon) golden rum
25ml hazelnut sauce
50ml whole milk
ice cubes
chocolate coin wrapped in gold foil

GLASSWARE

small milk bottle
–
You will also need
a blowtorch
or lighter

- Add the crushed ice to the small glass milk bottle until about three quarters full.
- Pour the amaretto, coffee liqueur, rum, hazelnut sauce and milk into a Boston shaker and add some ice cubes. Shake and strain into the milk bottle over the crushed ice.
- Slightly warm the milk bottle's rim using a blowtorch (it's fire, be careful!) or lighter. Remove one side of the foil from the chocolate coin and press the coin, chocolate-side down, on to the top of the milk bottle. The chocolate will melt slightly on the warmed glass, forming a lid. Allow to cool before serving.
- To serve, peel the remaining foil off the chocolate coin and stab through the chocolate lid with a metal straw.

SERIOUS

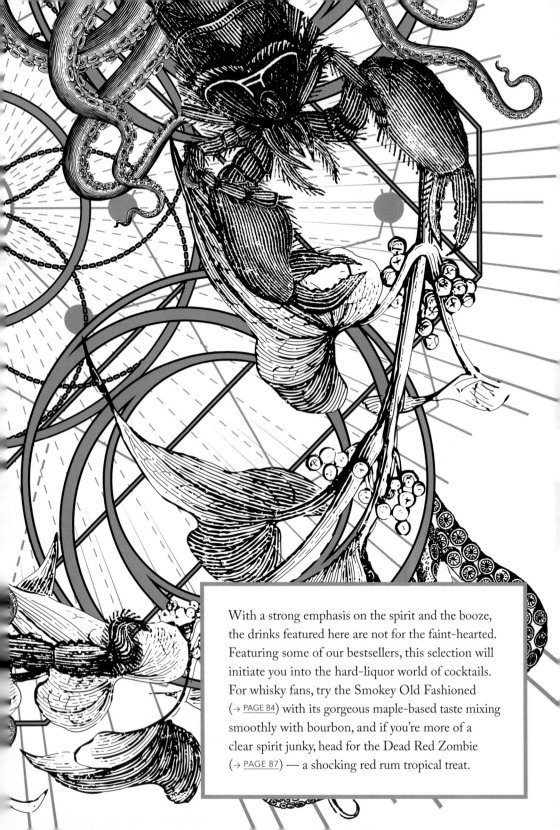

With a strong emphasis on the spirit and the booze, the drinks featured here are not for the faint-hearted. Featuring some of our bestsellers, this selection will initiate you into the hard-liquor world of cocktails. For whisky fans, try the Smokey Old Fashioned (→ PAGE 84) with its gorgeous maple-based taste mixing smoothly with bourbon, and if you're more of a clear spirit junky, head for the Dead Red Zombie (→ PAGE 87) — a shocking red rum tropical treat.

SMOKEY OLD FASHIONED

☛ **MAPLE, OAK, SMOKE**

We're super-fond of this signature drink, which has been on our menu from day one. Using maple syrup in place of demerara sugar, gives the mix a hint of smokey sweetness. Our pièce de résistance is to enhance the maple by smoking the mixture with woodchips before pouring over the ice.

MAKES 1
45ml bourbon
20ml maple syrup
1 dash of Bitter Truth Jerry Thomas Bitters
  or other aromatic bitters
25ml filtered water
ice ball

GLASSWARE

⧖

conical flask
rocks glass
—
You will also need
woodchips
and a smoke gun

- Pour the bourbon, maple syrup, bitters and filtered water into the conical flask and smoke with woodchips according to the instructions on → PAGE 10. Leave for a minute to infuse. Place the ice ball in the rocks glass and pour the infused mix over the top.

TIP

If you don't have a smoke gun at home, try adding a drop of smoked water to the liquid to achieve a similar smokey flavour, or enjoy without as a slightly sweeter twist on a classic Old Fashioned.

DEAD RED ZOMBIE

☞ SERIOUS, TIKI, TROPICAL

This may sound like the latest flick for horror fans, but in fact it's one of our favourite cocktails, a twist on a Zombie – a Tiki Classic from the 1930s. With a white rum base and tropical fruits, it's transformed into a shimmering zombie with a shot of our homemade Zombie Mix (→ PAGE 25).

GLASSWARE

zombie glass or small stein

MAKES 1

15ml (1 tablespoon) white rum
15ml (1 tablespoon) Wray & Nephew overproof rum
15ml (1 tablespoon) Grand Marnier
40ml pineapple juice
40ml cranberry juice
15ml (1 tablespoon) fresh lime juice
5ml (1 teaspoon) Zombie Mix → PAGE 25
ice cubes
75ml Fire Syrup → PAGE 30
½ passion fruit
2 pellets of dry ice (optional)

- Pour both rums into the glass, along with the Grand Marnier, pineapple juice, cranberry juice, lime juice and zombie mix. Add ice cubes and top with the fire syrup. Garnish with the passion fruit and top with the dry ice to serve. Do not drink the dry ice.

TIP

The dry ice adds an extra touch of theatre to this drink while moving the metallic powder around the glass, creating a shimmer effect. If you don't have dry ice at home, just give the drink a quick stir before serving to get a similar look.

LIFE'S A BEACH

👉 **WHISKY, BLOOD, SAND**

For those times when you're dreaming of a warm sunset
and the soothing sounds of waves lapping on the shore …
Whisky, vermouth and cherry liqueur star, while biscuit
crumbs feature on the rim to evoke a sandy beach.
Summertime living at its best.

MAKES 1

1 oaty biscuit, crushed

lime wedge

30ml whisky

5ml (1 teaspoon) maraschino cherry liqueur

15ml (1 tablespoon) Martini Ambrato
   vermouth or other white vermouth

15ml (1 tablespoon) L&G → PAGE 15

10ml (2 teaspoons) Simple Sugar Syrup → PAGE 28

40ml fresh orange juice

5 drops Red Mix → PAGE 30

GLASSWARE

coupe

- Place the crushed biscuit crumbs on a saucer. Glide
  a freshly cut lime wedge over the rim of the coupe and
  dip it in the biscuit crumbs so that they stick to the rim.
  Set aside.
- Pour the whisky, maraschino cherry liqueur, vermouth,
  L&G, sugar syrup and orange juice into a Boston shaker
  with some ice cubes. Shake and strain through a fine
  strainer into the biscuit-rimmed coupe. Drop 5 drops of
  red mix over the surface of the drink and serve.

SMOKEY NO. 2

☞ **SERIOUS, SMOKE, WINTER**

If you fancy a night nursing your drink over good conversation and classic tunes, then here's a treat for you. Calling for just a handful of ingredients, this fabulous cocktail is just two steps on from a rum Old Fashioned. Once smoked, it's served in a round-bottomed flask, ready to be lingered over and enjoyed long into the night.

MAKES 1
ice cubes
60ml dark golden rum
15ml (1 tablespoon) Winter Sugar Syrup → PAGE 29
20ml apple juice
cinnamon stick, to garnish

GLASSWARE

round-bottomed flask
—
You will also need
woodchips
and a smoke gun

- Put some ice cubes in a Boston shaker, then add the rum, winter sugar syrup and apple juice. Stir for 20 seconds to combine and dilute, then strain the liquid into the flask. Smoke with woodchips according to the instructions on → PAGE 10, and serve garnished with a cinnamon stick. It's too good to put down.

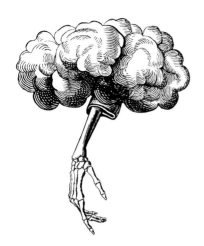

SHRUB A DUB DUB

👉 **TEQUILA, MINT, CITRUS**

Make merry with this fun and fruity cocktail, which we serve in a teacup. The harmonious blend of tequila, orange and grapefruit liqueurs with our homemade shrub means maximum flavour, with minimum fuss.

GLASSWARE

teacup, chilled

MAKES 1

ice cubes
30ml tequila
25ml Citrus & Mint Shrub → PAGE 29
15ml (1 tablespoon) Cointreau
15ml (1 tablespoon) pink grapefruit liqueur
juice of ⅙ fresh pink grapefruit
grapefruit zest twist, to garnish

- Put some ice cubes in a Boston shaker and add the tequila, shrub, Cointreau and grapefruit liqueur. Squeeze in the grapefruit juice and shake. Strain through a fine strainer into the chilled teacup and garnish with the grapefruit zest twist.

CHOCOLATE ORANGE SMASHERAC

☞ **CHOCOLATE, WHISKEY, GLASS**

Here's a serious and boozy tipple that will delight any cocktail connoisseur. We've had a little bit of fun with the absolute classic New Orleans Sazerac, which has been knocking around since the end of the 19th century. Once mixed, our slightly sweeter version is poured into a glass, then topped with an orange glass disc. Tap with a spoon to crack it and reach the elixir underneath.

MAKES 1
30ml bourbon
30ml cognac
10ml (2 teaspoons) Cointreau
10ml (2 teaspoons) chocolate cookie syrup
1 dash of chocolate bitters
1 dash of orange bitters
ice cubes
piece of Orange Glass → PAGE 34, to garnish

GLASSWARE

jam jar
or petri dish
—
You will also need
a spoon

- Pour the bourbon, cognac, Cointreau, syrup and both types of bitters into a Boston shaker along with some ice cubes. Stir for 30 seconds to mix and dilute, then strain into the jam jar and lay the piece of orange glass on top.
- Serve with a teaspoon and smash the orange glass and drink. Smashed it.

BANANAGRONI

☞ **BANANA, GIN, CITRUS**

A dead ringer for the classic negroni, with two twists. Swapping the Campari for Aperol provides a sweet element, while our homemade banana vermouth (see → PAGE 25) supplies the fruity punch. The overall taste is slightly sherbet-y. Best served with a dehydrated banana slice for a sophisticated finish.

GLASSWARE

rocks glass

MAKES 1
ice cubes
15ml (1 tablespoon) gin
15m (1 tablespoon) Aperol
30ml Banana Vermouth → PAGE 25
grapefruit zest twist
dehydrated banana slice, to garnish → PAGE 35

- Fill your rocks glass with ice, then add the gin, Aperol and banana vermouth. Stir for a few seconds.
- Squeeze the grapefruit zest twist over the glass to release its oils and aroma, then discard.
- Serve, garnished with a dehydrated banana slice.

PENICILLIN

 SMOKY, TANGY, MEDICINAL

Feeling a tad under the weather? Try our medicinal elixir, which will have you on the way to recovery in no time. It's one step on from a hot toddy, combining a 10-year-old whisky, a gorgeous marmalade vodka and a top-notch rich and spicy ginger liqueur.

MAKES 1
ice cubes
25ml Ardbeg Ten Years Old,
   or any peaty whisky
25ml marmalade vodka
15ml (1 tablespoon) L&G → <u>PAGE 15</u>
10ml (2 teaspoons) Simple Sugar Syrup → <u>PAGE 28</u>
10ml (2 teaspoons) ginger liqueur
cinnamon stick, to garnish

GLASSWARE

rocks glass
—
You will also need
a blowtorch

- Fill a Boston shaker with ice cubes and add the whisky, marmalade vodka, L&G, sugar syrup and ginger liqueur. Stir and strain into the rocks glass over some ice cubes.
- Use a blowtorch (it's fire, be careful!) to gently char the cinnamon stick, then add this to the drink as a garnish and serve.

FILTHY RICH

Celebrating a promotion, a bonus or a special
anniversary? If it's a big fat yes to any one of these, make
this unique cocktail. A super special golden sphere lies
at the heart of this glorious golden cocktail which brings
together a harmony of whisky, passion fruit syrup and
a couple of measures of champagne.

GLASSWARE

Nick & Nora
glass, chilled,
100ml beaker or
a small jam jar
—
You will also need
a spoon

MAKES 1

20ml Laphroaig whisky, or any smoky and peaty whisky
30ml passion fruit syrup
15ml (1 tablespoon) Citric Acid Dilution → PAGE 15
50ml champagne
ice cubes
1 Gold Vanilla Sphere → PAGE 33, to garnish

- Pour the whisky, passion fruit syrup, citric acid dilution
  and champagne into a Boston shaker with some ice
  cubes. Stir for 15 seconds, then strain with a julep strainer
  into the beaker or jam jar.
- Place the gold vanilla sphere in the chilled Nick & Nora
  glass and serve with a teaspoon, alongside the beaker
  or jam jar.
- To release the gold, use the teaspoon to pop the sphere,
  then pour the cocktail over the top.

NOSTALGIC

We've brought back the retro sweet shop vibe and the unmistakeable ring of the ice-cream van to offer you a celebration in nostalgia. Our creations here are inspired by our favourite suck-to-the-end sweets or chocolate bar (Rhubarb & Custard Sour anyone?), frozen dessert or your favourite bake — hello Key Lime Pie (on → PAGE 105). They're light-hearted, easy-drinking and not too boozy. So get ready to say hi to Paradise Lost (on → PAGE 102), Milk Lolly (on → PAGE 115) et al. and be prepared to be initiated into the world of these retro-inspired treats.

PARADISE LOST

👉 **TASTE OF PARADISE**

A clean-tasting, coconut-spiked cooler. Our version of
the classic chocolate bar, the Bounty, drink calls on a
gorgeous coconut rum and chocolate liqueur as the base,
then weaves them into the simple flavours of coconut
water, sugar syrup and lime. Top with a splash of soda
water to finish.

MAKES 1

1 lime wedge
2 teaspoons desiccated coconut
85ml coconut water
30ml coconut rum
25ml crème de cacao blanc (white chocolate) liqueur
15ml (1 tablespoon) Simple Sugar Syrup → PAGE 28
10ml (2 teaspoons) fresh lime juice
ice cubes
25ml soda water

GLASSWARE

collins glass

- Glide the lime wedge around the rim of the collins glass.
  Spread out the desiccated coconut on a saucer and dip
  the edge of the glass into the coconut to coat the rim.
- Pour the coconut water, coconut rum, crème de cacao
  blanc, sugar syrup and lime juice into a Boston shaker
  and shake.
- Place some ice cubes in the prepared collins glass and
  strain the mix over the ice. Top with soda water and serve.

KEY LIME PIE

 ZESTY, LIME, TART

Florida's favourite dessert is recreated in this superb, vivid green cocktail. The rim of crushed biscuits mimics the biscuit base, while the lime-y filling is zhuzhed up into a rum-based cocktail. A meringue swirl, toasted until golden, completes the treat. One to serve with a spoon!

GLASSWARE

coupe

—

You will also need a blowtorch or lighter and a spoon

MAKES 1
1 lime wedge
1 oaty biscuit, crushed
ice cubes
15ml (1 tablespoon) Midori melon liqueur
15ml (1 tablespoon) coconut rum
15ml (1 tablespoon) white rum
40ml apple juice
15ml (1 tablespoon) fresh lime juice
100ml Meringue Foam, to garnish → PAGE 19

- Glide the lime wedge around the rim of the coupe. Spread out the crushed biscuit on a saucer, then dip the edge of the glass into the crumbs to coat the rim.
- Fill a Boston shaker with ice cubes, then add the melon liqueur, coconut rum, white rum, apple juice and lime juice. Shake and strain into the coupe.
- Top with a swirl of the meringue foam. Use a blowtorch or lighter (it's fire, be careful!) to gently toast the meringue, then serve with a teaspoon.

CANDY CRUSH

POPPING, PINK, SILK

A frothy pink confection, featuring a fruity rhubarb and rosehip element. Sprinkle the popping candy carefully on top for the garnish in order to appreciate the full effect in your mouth as you start to sip away.

MAKES 1

45ml vodka
30ml rhubarb and rosehip cordial
30ml filtered water
20ml apple juice
5ml (1 teaspoon) grenadine
15ml (1 tablespoon) L&G → <u>PAGE 15</u>
25ml pasteurised egg white (or Vegan Foamer → <u>PAGE 15</u>)
3 ice cubes
½ teaspoon popping candy, to garnish

GLASSWARE

coupe

- Pour the vodka, cordial, water, apple juice, grenadine, L&G and egg white into a blender with the ice cubes. Blend for 30 seconds, or until the ice is completely blended.
- Strain into the coupe using a fine strainer to remove any remaining ice chips. Garnish with popping candy just before serving. Cracking…

SCREWBALL

Don't wait for the sun to shine before you rustle up this ice-cream inspired tipple. This cute little cocktail is one of our favourites all year round, and tastes just like a boozy, creamy bubblegum ice cream, thanks to a healthy splash of bubblegum-flavoured syrup. A mini swirl of white chocolate foam and a moreish maraschino cherry complete the act.

GLASSWARE

rocks glass

MAKES 1
ice cubes
25ml raspberry vodka
25ml blue curaçao
15ml (1 tablespoon) fresh lime juice
40ml apple juice
25ml bubblegum syrup
100ml White Chocolate Foam → PAGE 18, plus a small dome/swirl to garnish
maraschino cherry, to garnish

- Fill a Boston shaker with ice cubes, then add the vodka, blue curaçao, lime juice, apple juice, bubblegum syrup and white chocolate foam. Shake well. Add some ice cubes to the rocks glass, then strain the cocktail over the ice using a Hawthorne strainer.
- Top with a small swirl of white chocolate foam and a cherry to serve.

CHASE THE RAINBOW

CITRUS, RAINBOW, SKITTLES

This super refreshing cocktail of citrus flavours — think tart pink grapefruit and sweet oranges — is served in a wine glass with lots of ice to keep it chilled right down to the last sip. There's a bit of sparkle in there, too, from an equal dose of prosecco and soda water. It makes a lovely long summer drink.

MAKES 1
ice cubes
30ml pink grapefruit gin
15ml (1 tablespoon) Simple Sugar Syrup → PAGE 28
2 dashes of orange bitters
20ml pink grapefruit juice
50ml prosecco
50ml soda water
grapefruit zest twist, to garnish

GLASSWARE

wine glass

- Place some ice cubes in the wine glass, then add the gin, sugar syrup, bitters and grapefruit juice. Stir and top with the prosecco and soda water, then garnish with a twist of grapefruit zest to serve.

MALT-TEASER

☞ **MALT, TEXTURE, AIR**

There's bubbles aplenty here, just like the little round crunchy chocolates that inspired this cocktail. All the ingredients are dropped into a blender with ice, then whizzed at high speed to combine everything together. It's a really fun twist on the sweetie version, thanks to the hint of malt, a touch of cocoa and a couple of measures of liquor to hold it altogether.

GLASSWARE

coupe

MAKES 1

3 ice cubes
30ml crème de cacao blanc (white chocolate) liqueur
15ml (1 tablespoon) chocolate cookie syrup
15ml (1 tablespoon) golden rum
15ml (1 tablespoon) filtered water
25ml Malt Syrup → PAGE 30
1 dash of chocolate bitters
20ml apple juice

- Place the ice cubes in a blender, along with the crème de cacao blanc, chocolate cookie syrup, rum, water, malt syrup, chocolate bitters and apple juice.
- Blend until smooth, then strain through a fine strainer into your coupe.

LIQUORICE LADY

☞ **ANISEED, RASPBERRY, RETRO**

An uber grown-up version of every kid's favourite chewy sweet, Black Jacks. This is a clever mix of raspberry liqueur, lime juice and blue curaçao. For that unique dye-your-tongue-black effect while sipping, we drop a dash of food colouring into the mix before shaking everything together.

MAKES 1
ice cubes
40ml white rum
20ml raspberry syrup
15ml (1 tablespoon) fresh lime juice
15ml (1 tablespoon) blue curaçao
5ml (1 teaspoon) Zombie Mix → PAGE 25
¼ teaspoon black colouring powder

GLASSWARE

rocks glass

- Fill a Boston shaker with ice cubes, then add the rum, raspberry syrup, lime juice, blue curaçao, zombie mix and food colouring powder. Shake. Add some ice cubes to the rocks glass and strain the cocktail over the ice to serve.

MILK LOLLY

☞ **CHILDHOOD SUMMER HOLIDAY**

Here's one of our favourite fun cocktails — it really doesn't take itself too seriously at all! It has a creamy vodka base and tastes just like the milky ice lollies of your childhood. We serve it with a mini ice cream on the side. Definitely one for when the sun comes out…

GLASSWARE

🌿

coupe, chilled

MAKES 1
ice cubes
25ml vodka
25ml crème de cacao blanc (white chocolate) liqueur
10ml (2 teaspoons) vanilla syrup
100ml White Chocolate Foam → PAGE 18, plus a small scoop to serve
50ml soda water
mini ice cream cone, to serve

- Fill a Boston shaker with ice cubes and add the vodka, crème de cacao blanc, vanilla syrup and white chocolate foam. Shake, then strain through a fine strainer into the chilled coupe. Top with soda water to create a frothy texture.
- To serve, fill the mini ice cream cone with white chocolate foam to resemble a Mr Whippy and serve alongside the cocktail.

RHUBARB & CUSTARD SOUR

PUDDING, SWEETS, RETRO

The traditional elements of a sour — a spirit, some citrus and a dash of something sweet — are all here, but inspired by the retro rhubarb and custard sweet. There's a great vibe to this drink, with fruity rhubarb vodka and vanilla to give it that custard-y lilt. A twist of grapefruit tucked on top completes the party.

MAKES 1

ice cubes

30ml rhubarb vodka

15ml (1 tablespoon) Licor 43

15ml (1 tablespoon) L&G → PAGE 15

20ml pasteurised egg white (or Vegan Foamer → PAGE 15)

5ml (1 teaspoon) vanilla syrup

grapefruit zest twist, to garnish

GLASSWARE

rocks glass

- Place 3 ice cubes in a blender and add the vodka, Licor 43, L&G, egg white and vanilla syrup. Blend for a few minutes. Place some ice cubes in the rocks glass and pour the blended cocktail over the top. Garnish with grapefruit zest twist and serve.

TROPIC SWIRL

👉 **PASSION FRUIT, FRESH, SUMMER**

Your favourite summer lolly flavour… in reverse. Sip through the flourish of creamy white chocolate foam to reach the seductive and fruit-filled cocktail below. There's just the right level of acidity thanks to a squeeze of fresh lime, which balances the magical flavour combination of passion fruit, mango and orange.

MAKES 1
ice cubes
25ml passion fruit liqueur
25ml vodka
10ml (2 teaspoons) L&G → <u>PAGE 15</u>
15ml (1 tablespoon) fresh lime juice
40ml apple juice
40ml orange juice
10ml (2 teaspoons) mango syrup
½ passion fruit
75ml White Chocolate Foam → <u>PAGE 18</u>, to garnish

GLASSWARE

coupe, chilled

- Fill a Boston shaker with ice cubes, then add the passion fruit liqueur, vodka, L&G, lime juice, apple juice, orange juice, mango syrup and fresh passion fruit. Shake, then strain through a fine strainer into the chilled coupe.
- Top with a swirl of white chocolate foam and serve.

WIMBLEDON

🏴 **STRAWBERRIES, CREAM, DEUCE**

Boozy strawberries and cream in a glass. Make the most of one of our favourite summer berries with this bubblegum-pink cocktail. Choose super-ripe fruit, with an even red colour all over, for the best-flavoured garnish.

MAKES 1
ice cubes
25ml vodka
25ml strawberry liqueur
15ml (1 tablespoon) strawberry syrup
25ml strawberry purée
100ml White Chocolate Foam → <u>PAGE 18</u>,
   plus small dome to garnish
1 fresh strawberry, to garnish

GLASSWARE

rocks glass

- Fill a Boston shaker with ice cubes, then add the vodka, strawberry liqueur, strawberry syrup, strawberry purée and white chocolate foam. Add some ice cubes to the rocks glass, then strain the cocktail over the ice.
- Place the strawberry on the rim of the glass, topped with a swirl of white chocolate foam. Serve.

MINT CHOC

☞ **MALTY MINTY BUBBLES**

With inspiration drawn from the classic chocolate bar, this is a sophisticated little number and a particular treat for rum lovers. Creamy, malty, frothy — quite simply, a tasty drink.

MAKES 1
3 ice cubes
30ml crème de menthe blanc (white mint) liqueur
15ml (1 tablespoon) chocolate cookie syrup
25ml Malt Syrup → PAGE 30
20ml apple juice
15ml (1 tablespoon) golden rum
15ml (1 tablespoon) filtered water
24-carat-gold flakes, to garnish (optional)

GLASSWARE

coupe, chilled

- Place the ice cubes in a blender and add the crème de menthe blanc, chocolate cookie syrup, malt syrup, apple juice, rum and water. Blend for 30 seconds or until smooth and creamy, then pour into the chilled coupe to serve. Top with a pinch of gold flakes for an extra flourish.

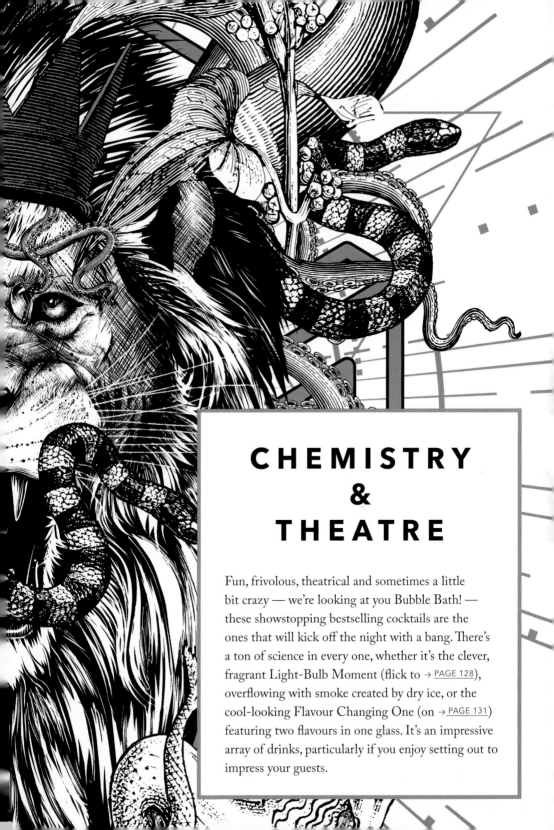

CHEMISTRY & THEATRE

Fun, frivolous, theatrical and sometimes a little bit crazy — we're looking at you Bubble Bath! — these showstopping bestselling cocktails are the ones that will kick off the night with a bang. There's a ton of science in every one, whether it's the clever, fragrant Light-Bulb Moment (flick to → PAGE 128), overflowing with smoke created by dry ice, or the cool-looking Flavour Changing One (on → PAGE 131) featuring two flavours in one glass. It's an impressive array of drinks, particularly if you enjoy setting out to impress your guests.

BUBBLE BATH

👉 **GIN, CITRUS, FAIRY LIQUID**

Remember the fun of filling your bath with bubbles for the Sunday night soak and watching it froth like crazy? Well, this little number features the same effect. It's gin-based, with a touch of raspberry Chambord and Aperol, but it's the reaction between the soy lecithin and the dry ice which creates this finish. Pink, bubbly, a lot of fun — and a bit of an institution at The Alchemist.

MAKES 1

ice cubes
30ml gin
30ml filtered water
10ml (2 teaspoons) Aperol
10ml (2 teaspoons) Chambord liqueur
15ml (1 tablespoon) L&G → PAGE 15
5ml (1 teaspoon) Simple Sugar Syrup → PAGE 28
20ml apple juice
½ teaspoon soy lecithin
2-3 pellets of dry ice

GLASSWARE

⧖

margarita coupe
or martini glass

- Fill a Boston shaker with ice cubes, then add the gin, water, Aperol, Chambord, L&G, sugar syrup, apple juice and soy lecithin.
- Shake for 30 seconds according to the instructions on → PAGE 8. Wet the coupe or martini glass slightly and add the dry ice pellets. Do not drink the dry ice. Use a muddler to compress, the pellets should stick to the bottom of the wet glass.
- Strain the cocktail through a fine strainer into the coupe or martini glass. Bubbles!

LIGHT-BULB MOMENT

☞ **FRAGRANT, SMOKING EXPLOSION**

Magical and mesmerising all at the same time, this
features plumes of smoke and a dramatic serve thanks
to a handful of dry ice. It's a fruity, summery drink,
combining gin, Pimm's, raspberry and ginger, and ranks
in our top five.

MAKES 1
25ml gin
25ml Pimm's No. 1
15ml (1 tablespoon) L&G → <u>PAGE 15</u>
15ml (1 tablespoon) raspberry syrup
100ml ginger beer
2 sprigs of mint
ice cubes
3 pellets of dry ice

GLASSWARE

rocks glass
light-bulb flask

- Place the gin, Pimm's, L&G, raspberry syrup, ginger beer
  and a mint sprig in a small saucepan. Simmer over a low
  heat until bubbles appear, then take off the heat.
- Place some ice cubes in the rocks glass and garnish with
  the remaining mint sprig.
- Place the dry ice in the light-bulb flask and strain in
  your liquid, creating ferocious plumes of fragrant smoke.
- Wait for the smoke to die down before pouring the
  concoction over the ice in your rocks glass. Do not drink
  the dry ice. Serve.

ICELESS MOJITO

☞ **FRESH, COLD, CURIOUS**

Science geeks at the ready! Our molecular mixology take on a mojito featuring mint-flavoured caviar and refreshing rum. The magic happens when the garden caviar is added to the drink, which bob around like wax in a lava lamp thanks to the bubbles in the dry ice.

MAKES 1
ice cubes
45ml white rum
25ml fresh lime juice
20ml Simple Sugar Syrup → PAGE 28
1 pellet of dry ice
5ml (1 teaspoon) Garden Caviar → PAGE 33

→ PAGE 28 → PAGE 33

GLASSWARE

100ml measuring cylinder or jam jar

- Fill a Boston shaker with ice cubes, then add the rum, lime juice and sugar syrup.
- Shake and strain through a fine strainer into the cylinder.
- Add the pellet of dry ice to the bottom of the measuring cylinder and add the garden caviar. Bubbles created by the dry ice will move around in the caviar. Do not drink the dry ice; wait for it to dissipate before drinking.

FLAVOUR CHANGING ONE

🚩 **WHAT'S YOUR FLAVOUR?**

A rather unassuming serve, that is, you start drinking.
In the glass, this looks completely clear — but as you sip,
the fresh raspberry taste gives way to a mint chocolate
flavour beneath. It's intriguing and clever at the same time.
A great one to trick unsuspecting guests.

GLASSWARE

rocks glass or jam jar

MAKES 1
50ml Flavour-changing Mix → PAGE 24
ice cubes
30ml raspberry vodka
25ml Citric Acid Dilution → PAGE 15
25ml filtered water
15ml (1 tablespoon) Simple Sugar Syrup → PAGE 28

- Pour the flavour-changing mix into the bottom your glass or jam jar, then fill the glass with ice cubes.
- Fill a Boston shaker with ice cubes, then add the raspberry vodka, citric acid dilution, filtered water and sugar syrup. Shake, then strain into the glass over the ice and flavour-changing mix. Do not stir. The layered liquid will create two contrasting flavours. Serve.

POT O'GOLD

☞ **GRAPEFRUIT, PINEAPPLE, JELLY**

Here's a fun one, and particularly good if you're looking
for a dash of pizzazz. Grapefruit and earthy rhubarb
spirits are matched together in the drink, which is then
served with a little pot — the gold! — of pineapple jelly
to enjoy alongside. It's boozy and very fruity.

MAKES 1
15ml (1 tablespoon) gin
15ml (1 tablespoon) rhubarb and ginger gin
15ml (1 tablespoon) L&G → PAGE 15
10ml (2 teaspoons) Simple Sugar Syrup → PAGE 28
juice of ½ fresh pink grapefruit
ice cubes
grapefruit zest twist, to garnish
1 serving of Boozy Pineapple Jelly → PAGE 35, to serve

GLASSWARE

rocks glass or beaker
—
You will also need
a spoon

- Add both types of gin to a Boston shaker, along with the
  L&G, sugar syrup, grapefruit juice and some ice cubes.
  Shake and place some ice cubes in the rocks glass and
  strain the cocktail over the top.
- Garnish with the grapefruit zest twist and serve with the
  pineapple jelly in its shot glass and a spoon on the side.

CARAMELISED RUM PUNCH

☞ **CARAMEL, SPICE, CARIBBEAN**

This take on a rum punch is a showstopper. Start by caramelising the sugar for a rich, mellow flavour, then pour in the Grand Marnier and flambé for a shot of instant theatre! Finishing with rum — naturally — along with watermelon syrup, pineapple and lime juice provides that totally tropical taste.

MAKES 1

2 teaspoons demerara sugar
15ml (1 tablespoon) Grand Marnier
pinch of ground cinnamon
pinch of ground nutmeg
30ml golden rum
25ml watermelon syrup
60ml pineapple juice
15ml (1 tablespoon) fresh lime juice
crushed ice, enough to fill your glass
cinnamon stick, to garnish

GLASSWARE

punch glass
or tankard
—
You will also need
a lighter

- Place a small saucepan over a medium heat and add the sugar. Heat until the sugar begins to caramelise (be careful, this will be incredibly hot), then add the Grand Marnier while still over the heat causing the Grand Marnier to ignite. Once flaming, sprinkle in the cinnamon and nutmeg, creating mesmerising sparks. Add the rum, watermelon syrup, pineapple juice and lime juice.
- Fill your punch glass or tankard with crushed ice and pour over the golden liquid. Serve, garnished with a cinnamon stick.

HOT & COLD ESPRESSO MARTINI

☞ **COFFEE, CREAM, SMOKE**

There's a little bit of trickery called for here with a mini milk bottle and the freezer, but the result is pretty special. Add in an aromatic coffee liqueur, a shot of espresso and a touch of drama, courtesy of dry ice, to deliver a unique twist on a classic.

MAKES 1
90ml double cream
20ml Simple Sugar Syrup → PAGE 28
30ml vodka
15ml (1 tablespoon) coffee liqueur
1 shot of espresso
25ml filtered water
2-3 pellets of dry ice

GLASSWARE

small milk bottle
with cap
(make sure your glass
is heat-proof)

- In a jug, stir together the double cream and half of the sugar syrup until completely mixed. Pour this mixture into the milk bottle and secure the cap tightly. Lie the bottle on its side in the freezer and freeze for 2 hours.
- Place a small saucepan over a medium heat and add the vodka, coffee liqueur, espresso, water and remaining sugar syrup. Simmer until completely heated through, but don't let the mixture boil. Transfer to a jug with a pourable spout.
- Remove the milk bottle from the freezer. The mixture should have frozen in place as the bottle was lying down, leaving one side of the bottle empty. Add the dry ice to the empty side.
- Carefully pour the hot mixture into the empty side, over the dry ice, creating large plumes of smoke. Serve with a reusable straw and allow the dry ice to dissolve before drinking. Do not drink the dry ice.

LEGAL ONE

☞ **HERBACEOUS, TROPICAL, CONTROVERSIAL**

We've had a bit of fun rustling up this one… the superior flavour comes via our own cardamom-infused herbaceous gin, homemade tropical vermouth, pineapple and coconut syrup and a splash of tonic for a little spritz. As the pièce de résistance, we like to serve it in a bong with a couple of pellets of dry ice, creating an impressive smoking finale.

GLASSWARE

🌿

bong or rocks glass

MAKES 1

30ml Cardamom Gin → PAGE 25
15ml (1 tablespoon) Tropical Vermouth → PAGE 25
1½ teaspoons fresh lime juice
50ml tonic water
15ml (1 tablespoon) filtered water
2 teaspoons pineapple and coconut syrup
ice cubes
2 pellets of dry ice
cardamom leaf, to garnish

- Pour the gin, vermouth, lime juice, tonic water, filtered water and pineapple and coconut syrup into a Boston shaker. Add some ice cubes and stir with a bar spoon for a few seconds – just long enough to mix and chill, but not to dilute.
- Place the dry ice in your glass or bong and carefully strain over the liquid. Do not drink the dry ice. Serve, garnished with a cardamom leaf.

CAVIAR ONE

☛ **QUINTESSENTIAL BRITISH CAVIAR**

A simple but showstopping way to pimp up your prosecco. The rhubarb caviar solution is squirted into a cocktail of rhubarb gin, citrus flavours and prosecco. With the aid of a little pellet of dry ice, the caviar bobs up and down in the drink.

MAKES 1

30ml rhubarb and ginger gin
10ml (2 teaspoons) Simple Sugar Syrup → PAGE 28
15ml (1 tablespoon) Citric Acid Dilution → PAGE 15
1 dash of lemon bitters
30ml prosecco
15ml (1 tablespoon) Calcium Solution → PAGE 14
ice cubes
1 pellet of dry ice
5ml (1 teaspoon) Rhubarb Caviar → PAGE 32

GLASSWARE

🍸

flute, chilled

—

You will also need
a pipette or syringe

- Pour the gin, sugar syrup, citric acid dilution, lemon bitters, prosecco and calcium dilution into a Boston shaker. Add some ice cubes and stir for 10 seconds, then strain into the chilled flute. Add the dry ice and serve with the rhubarb caviar liquid on the side in a pipette or syringe.
- To drink, slowly drip small droplets of the caviar mix into the drink until the pipette is empty. Do not drink the dry ice; wait for it to dissolve before drinking.

CLASSICS

If you're looking for a parade of quintessential cocktails, you've come to the right place. This collection of classics are all made from the same original recipes and time-honoured methods that have gone before. By dispensing with any twists and tricks and concentrating completely on the right measures within each drink, we've honed our recipes to ensure they deliver each and every time. Whether you have a penchant for an Espresso Martini (on → PAGE 154), laced with a splash of freshly made coffee, or you prefer an invigorating Bloody Mary (on → PAGE 147), known for its hair-of-the-dog qualities, you'll love this mixology repertoire.

AMARETTO SOUR

☞ **BISCUIT, CITRUS, SUMMER**

This almond-y delight is cut with our homemade
L&G citric flavour explosion and a drop of bitters to
soften the sweetness. We add a couple of ice cubes
into the mix in a blender, and this is where the magic
happens — it creates a wonderful velvety, fluffy texture
for you to enjoy as you sip away.

MAKES 1
2 dashes of aromatic bitters
25ml L&G → PAGE 15
45ml amaretto
25ml pasteurised egg white (or Vegan Foamer → PAGE 15)
ice cubes
lemon wedge, to garnish
maraschino cherry, to garnish

GLASSWARE

rocks glass

- Pour the bitters, L&G, amaretto and egg white into
  a blender and add 3 ice cubes. Blend until smooth
  and fluffy, then pour into the rocks glass filled with ice.
  Garnish with a lemon wedge and a maraschino cherry
  to serve.

MARGARITA

 **SALT, TANGY, LIME**

It's the fine layer of salt on the rim of the coupe glass that takes this cocktail to another level. While adding a savoury touch to the bitter-sweet orange liqueur, it also knocks back that slightly bitter edge brought by the tequila.

MAKES 1
2 lime wedges
sea salt flakes
25ml fresh lime juice
10ml (2 teaspoons) Simple Sugar Syrup → <u>PAGE 28</u>
50ml tequila
25ml Cointreau
ice cubes
or crushed ice

GLASSWARE

rocks glass, chilled
(for on the rocks)

coupe, chilled
(for straight up)

collins glass, chilled
(for frozen)

- Glide a lime wedge around the rim of the chilled glass. Spread out the sea salt flakes on a saucer, then roll the edge of the glass in the salt flakes to create a salt rim.

YOU HAVE THREE CHOICES FOR HOW TO MAKE AND SERVE YOUR MARGARITA.

ON THE ROCKS

- Pour the lime juice, sugar syrup, tequila and Cointreau into a Boston shaker. Add some ice cubes and shake well.
- Add some ice cubes to the salt-rimmed rocks glass. Strain the mixture through a fine strainer into the glass, then serve with a lime wedge on the rim.

STRAIGHT UP

- Fill a Boston shaker with ice cubes and add the lime juice, sugar syrup, tequila and Cointreau. Shake then strain through a fine strainer into the coupe. Garnish with a lime wedge on the rim.

FROZEN

- Add the lime juice, sugar syrup, tequila and Cointreau to a blender and add a cupful of crushed ice. Pour into the collins glass and garnish with a lime wedge.

BLOODY MARY

Famed for knocking a hangover on the head, this magical vegetable-rich cocktail is also ideal before Sunday lunch — it knocks the edge off your hunger pangs — and is a match made in heaven when served with a burger. This recipe makes a medium-spicy Bloody Mary, but feel free to ramp up the heat with extra Tabasco and Worcestershire sauce.

GLASSWARE

collins glass or
beer tankard

MAKES 1
35ml vodka
5 dashes of Worcestershire sauce
3 dashes of Tabasco
pinch of sea salt flakes
pinch of freshly ground black pepper
150ml tomato juice
juice of ½ lemon
ice cubes
celery stalk, to garnish
lemon wedge, to garnish

- Pour the vodka into your glass or tankard, followed by the Worcestershire sauce, Tabasco, salt, pepper, tomato juice and lemon juice. Stir well, then fill up the glass with ice cubes.
- Serve, garnished with a celery stalk and a lemon wedge.
- This recipe will create a medium heat, but feel free to add more or less spice to your taste!

TIP

Why not experiment with your garnishes?
Olives, pickles and cooked bacon all
make great choices, but the possibilities
are endless!

COSMOPOLITAN

☞ **SEX, CITY, ZEST**

It's the combination of lemon, orange, lime and cranberry that makes this bright pink cocktail a crowd-pleaser — well, that and the fact it was a big hit with Carrie Bradshaw et al. in the inimitable *Sex and the City*… We've kept true to the original recipe, finishing it off with a twist of flamed orange zest to release maximum flavour.

MAKES 1
ice cubes
40ml citron vodka
25ml Cointreau
40ml cranberry juice
15ml (1 tablespoon) fresh lime juice
orange zest twist

GLASSWARE
⌛
coupe, chilled
—
You will also need
a lighter or match

- Fill a Boston shaker with ice cubes, then add the vodka, Cointreau, cranberry juice and lime juice. Shake and strain through a fine strainer into the chilled coupe.
- Hold the orange zest twist over the glass and gently heat the zest with a lighter or match. As the heat draws the oil from the fruit to the surface, small sparks will start to emerge from the zest. Pinch the zest and flames will shoot out over the drink, creating a beautiful citrus aroma. Discard the zest before serving.

DEAD DIRTY MARTINI

☞ **FILTHY, SHARP, SHAKEN**

Can a dirty martini be made any better? We think so, with our Dead Dirty version — and we're sure you'll agree. The complexity of flavour comes from the aromatics in a slightly less-sweet vermouth, combined with a healthy measure of gin or vodka — you choose — and an olive. But it's the finishing touch of a syringe of olive brine served on the side that makes this extra special. Shoot in as much or as little as you desire…

GLASSWARE

❦

coupe or martini glass
—
You will also need
a syringe or pipette

MAKES 1
lemon zest
crushed ice
ice cubes
60ml vodka or gin
10ml (2 teaspoons) dry vermouth
10ml (2 teaspoons) olive brine, plus extra to serve
olive, to garnish

- Glide the lemon zest around the rim of the glass, then fill the glass with crushed ice and leave for a few minutes to chill. Discard the ice.
- Fill a Boston shaker with ice cubes and add the vodka or gin, vermouth and olive brine. Shake and strain through a fine strainer into the chilled coupe or martini glass.
- Fill the syringe or pipette with extra olive brine. Serve the martini, garnished with an olive, with the syringe of olive brine on the side.

PORN STAR MARTINI

☞ **CLASSIC, GLAMOUR, PASSION**

A sure-fire house party crowd pleaser... A relative newbie
on the bar scene, this has nonetheless well and truly
earned its place in the cocktail hall of fame.
All the classic elements feature: vodka, passion fruit
liqueur and pineapple juice, zhuzhed up with L&G,
our citrus-spiked syrup, and a dash of vanilla. A shot of
crisp prosecco served on the side makes this heavenly...

MAKES 1
ice cubes
30ml vodka
15ml (1 tablespoon) passion fruit liqueur
60ml pineapple juice
10ml (2 teaspoons) L&G → PAGE 15
5ml (1 teaspoon) vanilla syrup
1 fresh passion fruit, halved
brown sugar, for sprinkling
25ml prosecco

GLASSWARE

⧗

coupe, chilled
shot glass or conical
flask
—
You will also need
a blowtorch or lighter

- Fill a Boston shaker with ice cubes, then add the vodka,
  passion fruit liqueur, pineapple juice, L&G and vanilla
  syrup. Scoop out the pulp from one half of the passion
  fruit and add it to the mixture.
- Shake according to the instructions on → PAGE 8, then
  strain through a fine strainer into the chilled coupe.
- Take the remaining passion fruit half and sprinkle it
  with sugar, then use a blowtorch or lighter (it's fire,
  be careful!) to caramelise the sugar on the surface. Place
  the caramelised passion fruit in the centre of the glass.
- Pour the prosecco into a shot glass or conical flask and
  serve alongside the martini.

ESPRESSO MARTINI

☞ **COFFEE, LIQUEUR, SWEET**

So-called because it's the product of a shot of espresso combined with the vodka element of a martini. To sweeten it all up and marry these two soulmates together, we shake them hard with a coffee liqueur and a dash of sweet syrup.

MAKES 1
ice cubes
1 shot of espresso
10ml (2 teaspoons) Simple Sugar Syrup → PAGE 28
30ml vodka
15ml (1 tablespoon) coffee liqueur
3 espresso coffee beans, to garnish

GLASSWARE

⏳

coupe or martini glass, chilled

- Fill a Boston shaker with ice cubes and add the espresso, sugar syrup, vodka and coffee liqueur. Give it a hard shake and strain through a fine strainer into the chilled coupe or martini glass.
- Serve, garnished with three coffee beans.

VODKA MARTINI

☞ **ICONIC, DRY, BOND**

Shaken, stirred, wet, dry or dirty — there are many variations of this classic, served to suit the most discerning of drinkers. Our own favourite trick is to run a lemon zest around the edge of the glass, scenting it with a touch of citrus for the ultimate taste sensation.

GLASSWARE

coupe or
martini glass

MAKES 1
lemon zest
crushed ice
ice cubes
60ml vodka
10ml (2 teaspoons) dry vermouth
citrus zest of your choice, to garnish

- Glide the lemon zest around the rim of the glass, then fill the glass with crushed ice and leave for a few minutes to chill. Discard the ice.

☞ YOU CAN CHOOSE TO MAKE YOUR MARTINI WET OR DRY.

WET

- Fill a Boston shaker with ice cubes and add the vodka and vermouth. Shake (according to instructions on → PAGE 8) or stir, then strain into the chilled coupe.
- Garnish with your choice of citrus zest and serve.

DRY

- Pour the vermouth into a Boston shaker and add some ice cubes. Allow the vermouth to coat the ice, then strain out the vermouth, leaving the vermouth-coated ice cubes in the shaker. Now add the vodka and shake (according to instructions on → PAGE 8) or stir, then strain into the chilled coupe.
- Garnish with your choice of citrus zest and serve.

NEGRONI

Just like the cut of the finest suit in Milan, this Italian treat is sophisticated to the core. It's a straight and equal blend of gin, Campari and vermouth, and has to be mixed with ice very quickly so as not to water down the flavours. If you fancy experimenting, swap the gin for a double measure — that's 50ml — of chilled prosecco to create a Sbagliato.

GLASSWARE

rocks glass

MAKES 1
30ml gin
30ml Campari
30ml Martini Rubino vermouth or other sweet vermouth
ice cubes
orange zest twist, to garnish

- Pour the gin, Campari and vermouth into a rocks glass and fill the glass with ice cubes. Stir quickly to mix and chill, but try not to dilute the drink too much. Serve, garnished with an orange zest twist.

PALOMA

Sit down, draw up a stool and let us introduce you to the margarita's big sis, the paloma… This is a sophisticated and sunny amalgamation of tequila, freshly squeezed lime, grapefruit juice and a drizzle of agave syrup to take the edge off those sharp citrus flavours. A splash of soda completes the concoction, transforming it into a long and thirst-quenching cooler.

MAKES 1
ice cubes
45ml tequila
15ml (1 tablespoon) fresh lime juice
40ml grapefruit juice
5ml (1 teaspoon) agave syrup
75ml soda water
pink grapefruit wedge, to garnish

GLASSWARE

collins glass

- Fill a Boston shaker with ice cubes, then add the tequila, lime juice, grapefruit juice and agave syrup. Shake and strain into the collins glass.
- Top up with soda water to lengthen. To serve, garnish with the fresh pink grapefruit wedge.

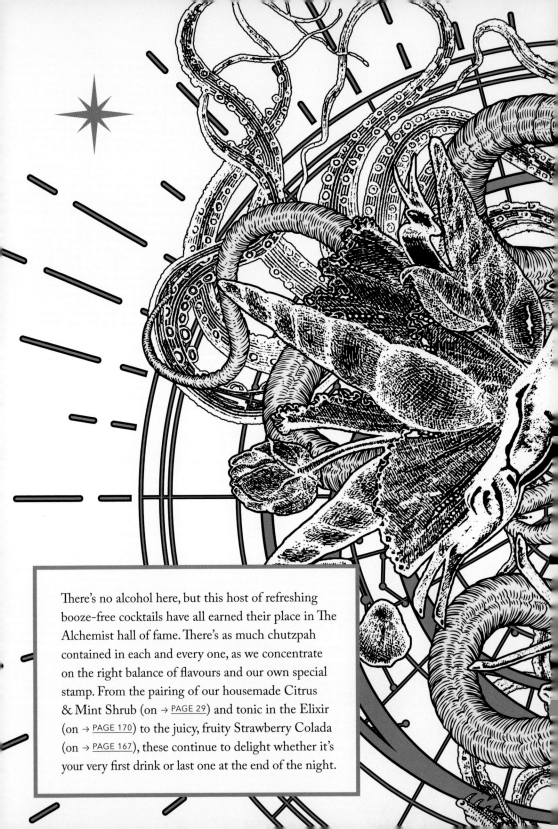

There's no alcohol here, but this host of refreshing booze-free cocktails have all earned their place in The Alchemist hall of fame. There's as much chutzpah contained in each and every one, as we concentrate on the right balance of flavours and our own special stamp. From the pairing of our housemade Citrus & Mint Shrub (on → PAGE 29) and tonic in the Elixir (on → PAGE 170) to the juicy, fruity Strawberry Colada (on → PAGE 167), these continue to delight whether it's your very first drink or last one at the end of the night.

BOOZE-FREE

MANGO SHAKE

☞ **TROPICAL, CREAMY, REFRESHING**

Think of this as a refreshing and grown-up twist on an American shake. Swapping the ice cream for a measure of white chocolate foam brings a decadent texture to this deluxe mélange of tropical fruit, sparkling soda water and a sidekick of citrus from our unique L&G syrup. It's creamy and thoroughly moreish, with a mouth-puckering dash of acidity from the freshly-cut passion fruit nestled on top.

MAKES 1
60ml apple juice
60ml orange juice
2½ teaspoons L&G → PAGE 15
10ml (2 teaspoons) mango syrup
1 fresh passion fruit, halved
50ml White Chocolate Foam → PAGE 18
ice cubes
25ml soda water

GLASSWARE

⧗

collins glass

- Pour the apple juice, orange juice, L&G and mango syrup into a Boston shaker. Scoop out the pulp from one half of the passion fruit and add it to the mixture. Finally, add the white chocolate foam and some ice cubes.
- Shake well. Add some ice cubes to the collins glass, then strain the cocktail through a fine strainer over the ice. Top up with soda water to create a frothy texture. Garnish with the remaining passion fruit half and serve.

BUBBLY GUM

☞ **BUBBLEGUM, CHILDHOOD, BUBBLES**

A fruit-tastic, booze-free cocktail matching all the flavours of the classic '70s bubblegum. It's pretty simple to knock up — just throw everything into a shaker, do your thing, then strain into a rocks glass over ice. For an effervescent frothy finish, drop a couple of cubes of dry ice into the glass just before serving.

GLASSWARE

❦

rocks glass,
conical flask or jam jar

MAKES 1

25ml bubblegum syrup
5ml (1 teaspoon) grenadine
40ml apple juice
40ml cranberry juice
15ml (1 tablespoon) fresh lime juice
½ teaspoon soy lecithin
ice cubes
3-4 pellets of dry ice ice

- Pour the bubblegum syrup, grenadine, apple juice, cranberry juice, lime juice and soy lecithin into a Boston shaker and add some ice cubes. Shake and strain through a fine strainer into a conical flask or jam jar.
- Fill the rocks glass with ice cubes and add place the dry ice pellets on top. Do not drink the dry ice. This will create bubbles when the cocktail mixture is poured over the ice. Serve.

OLLIE'S CUCUMBER SLING

 **ZESTY, GARDEN, REFRESHER**

Roll up, roll up, for this fab cooler… A spin on a traditional sling, this thirst-quenching number features apple juice, elderflower and chunks of chopped cucumber, all wrapped together in soda water. Pretty simple, yet very refreshing on a summer's day. Spike it with your favourite vodka or gin for a twist.

MAKES 1
ice cubes
50ml apple juice
25ml elderflower cordial
25ml L&G → PAGE 15
2.5cm piece of cucumber, chopped into chunks
soda water, to top up

GLASSWARE

sling glass

- Fill a Boston shaker with ice cubes and add the apple juice, elderflower cordial, L&G and chopped cucumber.
- Shake well and pour into the glass (don't strain). Top up with soda water and serve.

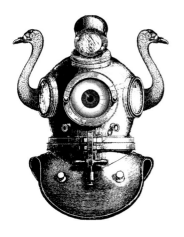

STRAWBERRY COLADA

☞ **TROPICAL, STRAWBERRY, CREAM**

If you like piña colada… you'll love our booze-free treat. Based on the classic recipe, this is conjured up by whizzing together luxurious coconut cream, strawberry purée, pineapple juice, a dash of grenadine — the sharp and sour pomegranate-flavoured syrup — with a squeeze of lime. It's a marbled delight and is crowned with fresh strawberries for a perfect finish.

GLASSWARE

🌿

collins glass

MAKES 1
crushed ice, enough to fill your glass
50ml coconut cream
70ml pineapple juice
15ml (1 tablespoon) fresh lime juice
25ml strawberry purée
5ml (1 teaspoon) grenadine
fresh strawberries, to garnish

- Add the crushed ice to a blender, along with the coconut cream, pineapple juice and lime juice. Blend for 30 seconds.
- Pour the strawberry purée and grenadine into the base of the collins glass, then hold the glass at an angle as you pour in the blended mixture. The final drink should have a marbled effect.
- Serve, garnished with strawberries.

KICK

ESPRESSO TONIC

Perfect for those times when all you need — or desire — is a pick-me-up, this sparkling effervescent cocktail is a favourite with our booze-free clientele, made from tonic water with a cap of espresso foam. It's served with a straw and sipped slowly, meaning the perfect balance of tonic and coffee is extracted from the glass.

MAKES 1
ice cubes
200ml tonic water
50ml Espresso Foam → PAGE 19

GLASSWARE

collins glass

• Place some ice cubes in the glass, then pour the tonic water over the top. Top with the espresso foam and serve.

ELIXIR

CITRUS, MINT, TONIC

Our homemade citrus and mint shrub is a powerhouse of flavour — an apple cider vinegar-based cordial, rustled up from segments of fresh orange and pink grapefruit, along with sprigs of fresh mint. This refreshing drink is served with a long cinnamon stick to stir, allowing its woody spice and subtle scent to infuse the aromatic concoction in the glass.

MAKES 1
ice cubes
40ml Citrus & Mint Shrub → PAGE 29
75ml tonic water
long cinnamon stick, to garnish

GLASSWARE

collins glass

- Place some ice cubes in your collins glass and pour the shrub over the top. Top with the tonic water and stir to mix. Serve, garnished with the cinnamon stick.

GLOSSARY

GLOSSARY

SODIUM ALGINATE

Alginate is a substance extracted from algae. It's known for its ability to hold water, making it a natural gelling agent. It's food safe and used as a thickening/gelling agent in jellies, ice creams, etc.

BITTERS

An alcoholic liquid flavoured with herbs and plants. Bitters were originally developed for medicinal purposes, but are now widely used as a cocktail ingredient.

CALCIUM LACTATE POWDER

Calcium lactate is a type of salt. It has various uses, including as a firming agent in some foods, but in molecular gastronomy it is used in the spherification and reverse spherification processes (→ PAGE 32 and → PAGE 33) because of the way it reacts with sodium alginate, causing a skin to form.

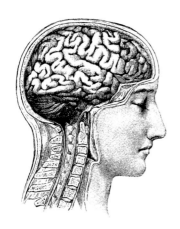

METHOCEL

A chemical compound deriving from cellulose. When blended with water, it forms a viscous, gel-like solution, and it can be used as a foaming agent. We use it in our Vegan Foamer (→ PAGE 15), an alternative to egg whites.

MSK ULTRAGEL

A vegan, seaweed-based gelling agent, this is perfect for use in jellies, such as our Boozy Pineapple Jelly on → PAGE 35.

SOY LECITHIN

A fatty substance deriving from soy, used as an emulsifier. We use it in our foams (→ PAGES 18-21) and cocktails to create a foamy, bubbly effect.

ULTRATEX POWDER

A gluten-free thickening starch.

XANTHAN GUM

Produced from simple sugars through a fermentation process, xanthan gum is used as a thickening agent in some of our foams and flavour mixes.

CITRIC ACID POWDER

Citric acid is found naturally in citrus fruits, especially lemons and limes. In its powdered form, it is used as flavour enhancer and can also be used as an emulsifying agent to prevent fats from separating. We use it in our Citric Acid Dilution (→ PAGE 15) as a way of adding a citrus flavour boost to a drink without affecting the colour or making the liquid cloudy in the way that adding fresh citrus juice will.

ISOMALT

A sugar substitute created from sucrose. It resists crystallisation, which makes it perfect for creating our crystal clear Orange Glass (→ PAGE 34).

MALT EXTRACT

A thick liquid syrup derived from barley grains and water. It has a sweet, distinctive flavour. We use it to create our Malt Syrup (→ PAGE 30).

COLOUR POWDERS

High strength food colourings which pack a powerful punch and mix well into almost any batch or liquid. A little bit goes a very long way.

FLAVOUR DROPS

Similar to essences which you would use in cooking, these flavour drops are intensely flavoured and provide a lot of flavour in very small amounts.

RESOURCES

SPECIAL INGREDIENTS

specialingredients.co.uk
Specialists in high-quality ingredients for molecular gastronomy and mixology.

MSK INGREDIENTS

msk-ingredients.com
Specialists in high-quality ingredients for molecular gastronomy and mixology.

SHOUT DRY ICE

shoutdryice.co.uk
Specialists in supplying dry ice to the catering industry.

BRISTOL SYRUP COMPANY

bristolsyrupcompany.com
High-quality syrups for your cocktails.

MONIN SYRUPS

monin.com
High-quality syrups for your cocktails.

BITTER TRUTH

the-bitter-truth.com
Bitters, liqueurs and spirits for cocktails.

SUGAR PAPER SUPPLIER

thecakedecoratingcompany.co.uk
Design your own sugar paper pieces here to use as creative garnishes.

CREAM CHARGER & N20 CARTRIDGE SUPPLIER

specialingredients.co.uk
Specialists in supplying chargers and cartridges to the catering industry.

WOODCHIPS SUPPLIER

halenmon.com
A useful online resource for woodchips.

INDEX

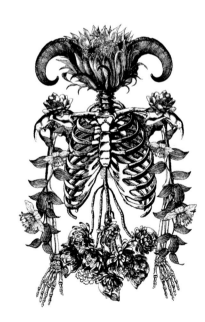

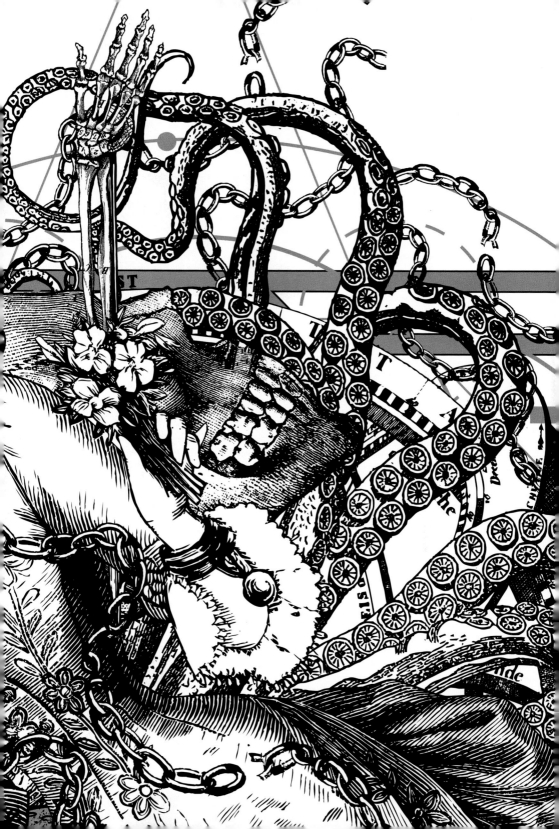

ACKNOWLEDGMENTS

This book is dedicated to the creativity, character and passion of Alchemist bartenders, past and present – there are too many names to list individually, but our first and most special thanks must go to Felix, the beating heart and the lightening rod through which everything flows on our bars – from drinks to drainage and everything in between, and without whom, this book could not have existed.

Over the last 10 years there have been some remarkable individuals who have helped to create our cocktail culture and we are grateful for the dedication of each and every one of them, but there are 3 whom have transcended all excellence. Holly whose devotion to the evolution and elevation of each drink that makes its way onto our menu; Elliot for his tireless energy in spreading the message of the craft and the joy of bartending across the land; and to Sam, who does the real hard work, and just Gets. It. All. Done.

Along with Adam and Ste, we want to show our utmost appreciation to Ray, ably assisted by Greg, Dariush & Ben, who lit the first flames of Alchemy in 2010 and set the benchmark for the drama that followed.

A shout to Kieran, the quick witted voice of The Alchemist, for the amplification and celebration of our drinks – helping to send love and theatre beyond the 4 walls of our bars and into the annals of history; curating the beautiful images and spreading the good work through our brand channels.

A big thanks to Jenny who had the unenviable task of herding the Alchemist bartending cats together in order to pull this off and has painstakingly curated the beautiful recipes and images contained in these pages. Her sorcery course through The Alchemist in all its guises but her real magic is her desire to never accept anything less than perfection and without her, this book *would* not have existed.

We are grateful to Camilla and all at Penguin for all their guidance and input into making this book the very best it could be and with the help of Jamie and the team at Vapour, whose inspired and innovative imagery have helped us achieve this remarkable memorial to the last 10 incredible years in our bars.

We've indexed a number of suppliers to help you create and craft at home, but would like to say particular thanks to Mike at Shout Dry Ice; Danny at Ashro; Laura & Vicky at MSK; Dan at Special Ingredients; Kev on the lemons and limes and all at 200 degrees for the brilliant beans.

Finally and sadly, we pay tribute to the late, great, Tim Bacon – The Alchemist is his brainchild and we hope he looks down proudly on his impossible dream. You can read more about Tim, his remarkable life, and the important legacy he leaves behind at *www.timbaconfoundation.co.uk*.

Love and Theatre x

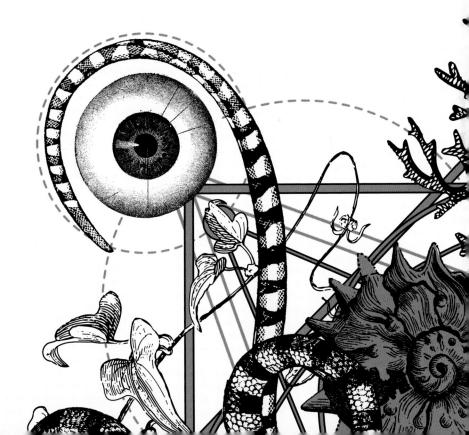

Published in 2021 by Ebury Press, an imprint of
Ebury Publishing,
20 Vauxhall Bridge Road,
London SW1V 2SA

Ebury Press is part of the Penguin Random House group
of companies whose addresses can be found at global.
penguinrandomhouse.com

Photography: Haraala Hamilton
Assistant Food Stylist: Sarah Vassallo
Prop Stylist: Rachel Vere
Design (interior pages): Sandra Zellmer
Illustrations: Vapour
Production: Sian Pratley
Editor: Camilla Ackley

This edition first published by Ebury Press in 2021

www.penguin.co.uk

A CIP catalogue record for this book is available from
the British Library

ISBN 9781529107951

Printed and bound in China by Toppan Leefung ltd

Penguin Random House is committed to a sustainable future
for our business, our readers and our planet. This book
is made from Forest Stewardship Council® certified paper.